The 150 Years

D1363052

A History of the
St. Andrews Golf Club
1843 to 1993

by Eric D. Clark

Printed by QUICK PRINT, St. Andrews

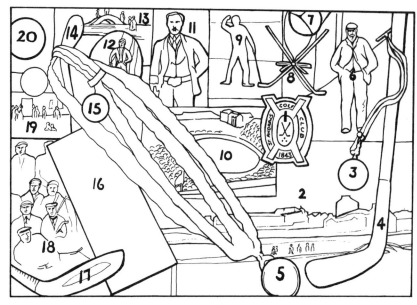

KEY TO COVER

1   St. Andrews Club Blazer Badge
2   The Home Hole 1843
3   Tom Morris Jnr's. Watch and Chain
4   Cleek, Circa 1860
5   The Captain's Trophy and Chain 1846
6   Tom Morris Snr. Open Champion 1861•62•64•67, Honorary Member of the Club
7   Feather Ball 1843. Made by Robertson / Morris
8   Crossed Clubs (1850), runner up prize to Captain's Trophy
9   Ballesteros, "Salute to the Club!" The Open 1984, (Photograph by club member Lawrence Levy)
10   "View from the Club Roof" Faldo's winning of the 1990 Open, (Photograph by Club member Masakuni Akiyama)
11   Tom Morris Jnr. Open Champion 1868•69•70 & 72
12   Allan Robertson - past captain, known as "The World's First Professional"
13   Swilken Bridge 1857, "Playing to the First Green" (now the 17th)
14   A Hugh Philp Playclub 1856
15   Gutta Ball 1850 - Hand Rolled
16   St. Andrews Club Fixture List 1992
17   Allan Robertson Playclub 1843
18   Members of the club team of 1897
19   "The Auld Union Parlour" the first clubhouse in St. Andrews
20   The Gutta Ball used by Allan Robertson for the record score of 79 on the Old Course 1857

Cover devised and designed by club member David Joy • *Photograph by Ian Joy Photographic*

TABLE OF CONTENTS

FOREWORD

Golf Club histories do not normally make for lively reading. Often you can find the same level of interest perusing a Telephone Directory or a Cookery Book. They tend to occupy shelves rather than minds.

I have tried to make this book readable both for members and to other golfers outwith the club.

The first two chapters set the golf scene in St. Andrews in 1843 and the following fifty years when the foundations of our modern game were laid down.

The remaining chapters tell the story of St. Andrews Golf Club largely as revealed in the Minute Books. I do not apologise for quoting extensively from them because the Victorian phraseology gives the extracts their own special flavour.

Throughout I have tried to bring out the human and humorous side of this great Club's development.

Every author accumulates is own "Thank you" list.

My greatest debt is owed to the three previous Club historians - John Sorley (1911), Robert Baptie (1933) and Andrew Bennett (1946). Without their researches life would have been very difficult for me.

David Joy has made a major contribution. Many of the old photographs and all the line drawings of our champions are his, as is the cover design. Throughout he has been enthusiastic, supportive and knowledgeable.

Reading my handwriting is an art which Mrs. Judy Cox acquired in long hours of transcribing. She was patient and encouraging, above and beyond the call of duty.

My wife, Kay, was of great help in proof reading the pages just before printing. Terry Scanlon of Quick Print handled the printing of the history.

Thanks are due to two Companies. GB Papers, Guardbridge provided the paper as they also did for our Centenary History in 1946. St. Andrews Golf Club looks forward to them providing the paper for our Bicentenary history in 2043.

Howard Smith Papers (Scotland) Ltd. provided the financial back-up which allowed us to tackle the production of this history.

I and St. Andrews Golf Club thank the two companies and all those who helped to make this book possible.

Eric D. Clark (November 1992)

ST. ANDREWS IN 1843

What kind of town was the St. Andrews in which our founder members lived? Its houses still were grouped around the three main streets of old - North Street, Market Street and South Street. Just beyond the West Port lay the "suburb of Argyle."

It had become a sleepy, decaying backwater - the grand days of three hundred years before were only a memory. A history of the town written in 1849 reported "Amid crumbling walls and green clad streets, the citizens lived in contented ease and hopeless indifference." Their indifference was shaken when Hugh Lyon Playfair became Provost in 1842. For the next nineteen years he set about the crumbling town and by 1861 had cleaned it up and set in motion the Victorian building boom which gave us the elegant terraces and public buildings which are so attractive. Playfair was not short of challenges.

Contemporary reports tell of the numerous dung hills, cow houses, pig sties and the open sewers in the streets. The stench must have been noticeable! Weather statistics of the day record 25 calm days. The inhabitants probably welcomed the other 340 days when the winds blew and kept the aromas moving on. Doubtless, the fair winds which freshened the town's streets and wynds often proved to be unfair winds for the golfers struggling through the whin lined links on the shore.

The population was around 4000. A breakdown of the occupations revealed 85 gentry and professional men, 42 shopkeepers, 394 tradesmen, 49 day labourers and 57 seamen and fishermen.

Our founder members were mostly tradesmen, who at that time earned about 12/ - to 16/- per week. The weavers, day labourers and fishermen earned 6/- to 12/- per week. The one industry mentioned was golf ball making. Allan Robertson had a thriving business. It is estimated that about 10,000 feathery balls were made in the town per year, around half for local use. They cost around 2/- each. When you set that against the 1/4d to 1/6d per day earned by a casual labourer you realise that golf was not a poor man's game in 1843.

The wealthier folk tended to live in South Street, the less well to do in Market Street and North Street. Life was hard for the poor - it always is. Large families were brought up in earthen floored rooms the size of a modern garage. There was no running water and the food was basic indeed - oatmeal and potatoes, wheaten bread and oatcakes, broths and pork, salt herring and fresh fish.   Tea was a luxury.

Whisky was not!   Around 12,000 gallons were sold annually, half from the grocers' shops, half from the twenty-four public houses in the town.   In addition, there were eleven premises licensed to sell ales and porter only.

Reports of the day tell with disapproval of the drunkenness among the fishing families but perhaps if we think of them having to net a living in open sailing boats among the storms of the German Ocean, we can show them rather more sympathy. Traditionally some of the fishermen helped out their scanty earnings by working as caddies.

Cholera and typhoid were still lurking in the background, bronchitis and rheumatism were common ailments. But the same reports comment on how healthy life was in the town and gives golf some credit for this.

"The amusement of golf, which is general with all ranks, is the best prophylactic in preventing dyspepsia and hypochondriasis which occasionally occur." There may be something in the claim. Do you know any golfers who suffer from hypochondriasis?

Sometimes, perhaps often, the best aspect of a round of golf is the opportunity it provides for sitting down with friends over a drink when the game is ended.

By the year 1843 all kinds of controversial and talk-worthy events were taking place. Our first members had plenty to discuss and argue about, apart from missed putts and lost balls.

The political situation was tense. The Chartist movement was still rumbling on. Its supporters were looking for basic political rights such as the vote for everyone and secret ballots. About this time some of the Chartists leaders were tried and deported to Australia because of their dangerous views.

In the Highlands, the Clearances still continued.   The glens were gutted, their people shipped off to North America and Australia, and replaced by the money making sheep.

The Scottish Church was split wide open by the Disruption of 1843. Forty percent of ministers and congregations broke away from the established church, demanding the right to appoint their own ministers and not have them imposed on their churches by patrons, often the local landowners.

There was another revolution to talk about - the Railway Revolution. It is difficult for us to comprehend how remote St. Andrews was before 1843. It was only in 1829 that the first stage coaches began to go from the town - once a week to Cupar, twice a week to Dundee.

But by 1848, six thousand navvies had driven the new railway line across Fife from Burntisland to Tayport. Three years later the railway came to St. Andrews and a new era was born. Suddenly a door to the world outside was opened for St. Andreans and through the same door came ever increasing numbers of golf enthusiasts to visit the "Capital of Golf Land."

Balfour described his rail journey from Edinburgh to St. Andrews in the 1850's thus:

"To begin with there was no Forth Bridge in existence and the journey from Edinburgh was a tedious and slow one. You took the train as you do today (i.e. 1904) at the Waverley Station and you crawled slowly on to Granton There you left the train and got into a little steamer that was to take you across the Firth of Forth. Sometimes the passage was made in perfect weather and then the sail across was a welcome relief from the stuffy and slow train. But more frequently the weather was stormy and boisterous and the crossing was horrible in every way. You were glad to reach Burntisland and get into the train again though you knew it was a North British one and the slowest of the slow. You had to change carriages and often have a long and tedious wait at Ladybank. Thence on to Leuchars where you had to change again."

As a boy he found the journey a slow one. It would have been a lot slower on foot or horse back!

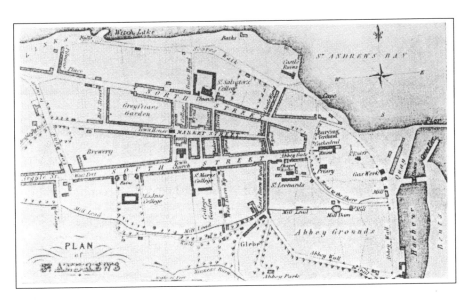

Street plan of St. Andrews in 1845 (from Fletcher's Guide to St. Andrews, 1845)

North Street "Ladyhead" Fisherwomen

The Home Hole 1854 (1st Railway Station in background)

8

GOLF AND GOLFERS
1843-1900

THE OLD COURSE

Town records from the 1540's mention the employment of two old ladies to look after injured golfers. In those days more than the golfer's pride required to be repaired.

By the time our Club was formed the Old Course was already very old. What kind of course did our founder members play on? Certainly modern players would be shaken to the core if asked to battle their way through the whins and sands and heather and then putt out on the roughly formed greens which faced the enthusiasts of 1843.

Balfour wrote his "Reminiscences of Golf" at the end of last century. He covered the period from 1842 when he joined the R&A until 1887. Even in those 45 years he could record substantial changes in the Old Course - none of which he conceded was an improvement.

In his day there must have been talk about converting the course to the circular layout which we know because he speaks very scathingly of the suggestion, pointing out that "it would have deprived parties of meeting their friends and hearing how their matches were getting on." Even the innovation of cutting two holes on each green (i.e. one for outgoing and one for incoming players) upset him, considering that it had taken much of the interest away from the game.

In 1754 when the R&A was formed there were 22 holes. The course was shortened to 20 in 1756 and by 1843 it was reduced to 18 - nine out and nine back. We can all be thankful that the 22 hole golf course did not become the one adopted for posterity!

The convention in those days was that when two games were approaching a hole from opposite directions, the group reaching the green first had priority. One can imagine some sharp exchanges over which group should stand aside.

Balfour describes how, in the 1840's, the 17th green was in fact the 1st green. The shot into the green negotiating the Swilcan, the bunker and the road must have been a testing one.

The second hole playing up our 17th fairway was also difficult.   On the left, alongside the wall were belts of rushes. At the corner, between the wall and the bunkers, were dense whins making the hole a dog leg requiring players to go onto the present second fairway.

The third (now the 16th) had whins along the left where the railway line was to

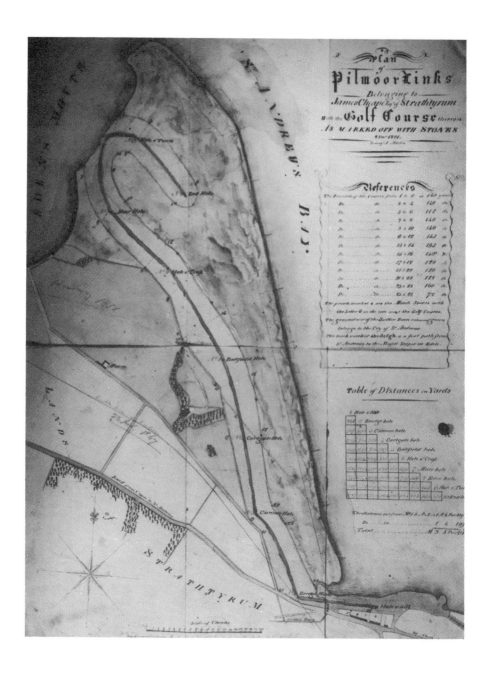

1821 Map
In 1754 the Old Course had 22 holes which were reduced to 18 in 1764.
The greens were enlarged to have two holes on each in the 1830's.

run and rough grass down the right. Equally tight was the 4th hole.

Hell bunker was negotiated on the right. The second shot was to the left up onto the Elysian Fields (now the 14th fairway) which was "short and smooth like a putting green". The third shot had to avoid the Beardies and the fourth shot to the green was across a "wide, staring, horrid bunker."

Before improvement later in the century the 6th green was bare and the putting surface made up of earth, heather and shells - not the ideal surface in any century.

The hidden bunkers which now catch what seem accurate drives from the present 12th tee, only make sense when you look back at them from the 12th green and realise that they were designed for play going out to the Eden estuary, not coming away from it.

The ninth or end hole is much the same as the one we play but formerly was thick with heather and whins which once negotiated getting to the green had to be recrossed on the first of the inward nine holes.

Balfour speaks very highly of the 13th hole as it was then laid out, describing it as the most difficult on the links. "Improvements", which removed the dense whins and bunkers protecting it, have drawn its teeth but before that even the great Allan Robertson played it very cannily as a three shotter to avoid disaster.

The 18th hole was a tougher proposition. In the 1840's the green was "on broken ground in a hollow with the ground sloping down on both sides." Earlier in the century the sea had come up to where the steps from the R&A now are and sand dunes ran alongside the last green. The last green, as we know it, came later with the "formation of an artificial table land."

Tom Morris came back from Prestwick in 1864 at the invitation of the R&A to supervise the links. He introduced heavy rollers and grass cutting machines and water to the greens. Whins were torn out to widen fairways. Another innovation was to provide sand boxes for the teeing off areas and metal cups to define the holes. Perhaps the one advantage our predecessors had in 1843 was that the holes were bigger. Often sand was taken out of them for setting up the ball for the next drive - which must have made them increasingly wider and deeper.

The holes were marked with a small iron pin with a piece of red flag attached. After holing out, players had to tee off within eight club lengths of the previous hole - surely a dangerous pursuit with golf balls coming into the replaced pin from both directions.

The problem must have been even greater in 1744 when the green was defined as the ground one club length around the hole. By 1777 this was enlarged to four club lengths from the hole. 1828 saw the green extended to eight club lengths from the hole.

Tom Morris
1850

11

The Swilken Burn
Allan Robertson, on the bridge, is watching his partner play to the first green
(i.e. the present 17th green). Tom Morris is on the left.

Allan Robertson (with his club on his shoulder) with a group of his contemporaries.
Tom Morris is to the right, Willie Park is behind on the left and Willie Dunn is addressing the ball (1857)

12

Although the greens became bigger it was a long time before their quality improved. Even in 1896, W. Park, Jnr., in his book "The Art of Putting" was giving advice on how to putt out of a bad lie!

Fortunately for players of the day congestion on the Old Course was not a problem and golfing life was much more leisurely and relaxed. One description of the early scene talks of "Sir John Low of Clatto, riding on his cream coloured pony and dismounting to play when his turn came in his foursome."

If games finished early some players would have a refreshment at the 15th (the "Ginger Beer Hole" and now the name for the 4th hole) and start their second round from the 5th hole. Of an evening after work Allan Robertson and Tom Morris and their cronies would go out for friendly games, playing for a glass of "Black Strap" (stout or porter) enjoyed in the Union Parlour.

And over the drinks the same old stories - "In the evening each dilates on his own wonderful strokes, and the singular chances that befell him in the different parts of the green! - all under the pleasurable delusion that every listener is as interested in his game as he is himself."

GOLF BALLS

Our first members played with 'featheries'. Allan Robertson made his living making them, helped by Tom Morris. His cottage and workshop was on the corner of The Links and Golf Place - a stone's throw from our present Club house.

The balls were made from three pieces of leather stuffed usually with poultry feathers compressed into the casing which was then stitched. Tom Morris who worked for Allan Robertson, when talking of his trade, said "You were just a kind of shoe maker." The balls themselves were usually more egg shaped than round and must have presented problems when putting. A contemporary piece of doggerel described them thus:-

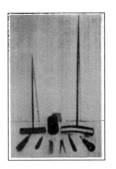

Instruments used in making a feather ball. Two awls with wooden chest braces, one leather ball-holder, two short awls, two wooden feather stuffers, one pair of callipers, and a strip of leather.

> "And though our best with them we tried
> And nicely every club applied
> They whirred and fuffed and dooked and shied
> And sklentit into bunkers"

But in 1843 a golf ball revolution was in the making. The gutta percha was a Malaysian tree which yielded a juice which hardened in air. Within five years it had been made into balls and used on a golf course.

The gutta percha was softened in hot water, then hand rolled into a ball. The new ball was half the price of a feathery and lasted indefinitely.

It was not long before golfers noticed that hacked balls appeared to fly better than smooth ones. Thereafter the balls were deliberately scored by hammer and finally

"THE AULD UNION PARLOUR" 1851

Used as the Club House before the R. & A. Clubhouse was built. Hamilton Hall now occupies this site

produced in moulds with the regular indentations in the mould.

The same versifier could write of the new ball:
"Ye're keen and certain at a putt
Nae weet your sides e'er open up
And though for years your ribs they whip
Ye'll never moutt a feather"
Small wonder he could proclaim
"Hail gutta percha precious gum".

The new balls very quickly came into fashion and the St. Andrews Club offered four of them as prizes in an 1851 Medal. Sadly they were the cause of a break up between Allan Robertson and Tom Morris. The latter had been tempted to try the new gutta percha ball and his employer Allan, seeing his livelihood threatened, took umbrage. Even he had to change and start producing the new ball.

By the 1870's all kinds of composite balls were being made from gutta percha mixed with ground cork and metal filings sometimes with a lead weight in the centre. One of the golf ball pioneers was Captain Stewart of St. Andrews who produced a wound elastic ball with a gutta percha cover. Some 30 years later the Haskell ball was produced using the same principle. Sandy Herd won the 1902 Open playing the new Haskell ball.

GOLF CLUBS

Around 1843, the numbers of clubs carried by players were limited. Some golfers made do with three - a driver, a lofting iron and a putter. Most of the clubs were woods with heads made from beech or applewood. The new hard gutta balls caused problems and the faces were reinforced with leather or vulcanite inserts. Putting lead weights in the balls aggravated the problem - small wonder that Hugh Philp, one of the town's early club makers, was driven to complain "How the devil can a man make clubs to stand against lead?"

A range of wooden clubs gradually evolved. The Play club was the driver and the grassed (or lofted) driver was the forerunner of our No 2 and 3 woods.

There were various spoons - the Long Spoon, the Middle Spoon, the Short Spoon and the Baffing Spoon, sometimes called the Cutty. The last named was designed to throw the ball up into the air and was most effective when playing the feathery ball.

Balfour in his "Reminiscences of Golf" becomes quite lyrical when talking of the fast disappearing Baffing Spoon. He says "It is used when near the hole and when the ball has to be lifted over a hazard or uneven ground. There are few prettier strokes in the game. The ball is tossed high in the air and hovers for a moment, as if to choose what blade of grass to alight on, then drops, and does not run above a foot or so."

Around mid century the iron clubs used were usually the driving iron or cleek, and the small headed rut iron designed to howk balls out of bad lies - of which there must have been many. Allan Robertson is said to have been one of the first players to use the cleek regularly. Balfour was not pleased - "It is said that Allan Robertson introduced the use of the cleek when near the hole. If so, it is, I think, a pity that he did. It is not so pretty a stroke; it destroys the green, as some even intentionally cut the turf with it; and it is not more sure than the stroke with the 'Baffy'."

Towards 1890 the old range of wooden clubs began to be replaced with two new ones - one was the Wooden Niblick, "a long spoon with a very short head, plated with brass on the bottom from which it gets its other name of the 'Brassy'." It was designed for moving a ball lying badly. The other innovation was the bulger. This wood had a shorter, rounded head with a deeper face which was slightly convex.

In "The Golf Book of East Lothian" by Kerr (1896) Sandy Herd described his golf set thus:

"My driver is a bulger with a nice round face not too much bulged, and is of wood. I do not think any substitutes proposed for wood, and I have tried them all, will do. I generally put a piece of leather in the centre of the face of my driver, as it makes the face last longer, and I think helps the length of the drive. The shaft of my driver is stiffish..... My brassie is also a bulger, a little bit shorter in shaft than the driver with a smaller head so as to get at a cupped ball... My cleek is of the ordinary kind, no patent long-driving affair, for it drives far enough for my purpose. I use two irons, one a medium, with a good bit of 'loft' on it, the other more straight in the face which I find very useful for playing against the wind or for approaching the hole when the medium won't carry sufficiently far. My mashie is an ordinary one with a good big head and a lot of pitch on it. I find this club very useful. It has a stiff shaft: with a supple shaft one can't make the ball stop so 'dead' as with a stiff one."

Sandy Herd went on to say "Then as to the putter, I count it the most important club of the set - I change my putter frequently." His clubs certainly served him well and with them he won The Open in 1902. He joined our club in 1886 and was the first winner of the R&A's Gold Medal in 1890. The same year the R&A's Secretary questioned his amateur status but our Committee rejected the complaint.

THE IRON AGE

Sandy Herd

The first half of the 19th century was very much the "Wooden Age", while the second half can be described as the "Iron Age" and the revolution dates from 1848 when the gutta ball appeared. A mis-hit with an iron on a feathery ball was expensive and often terminal. A badly hacked gutta could be put into hot water, rolled out and be made as good as new.

A set of clubs from before 1800, on display at Troon Golf Club, has six woods and two irons. The two irons were 'desperation' clubs and only used in emergency situations.

The first was the small headed, deep faced iron called the track iron or rut iron, and the other the "Iron", which seems to have been used when looking for distance from dubious lies. The "Iron's" toe was either squared off or rounded.

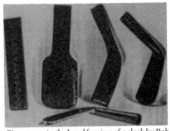

Five stages in the hand forging of a cleek by Bob Wilson of St. Andrews.
(Collection, the Royal and Ancient Golf Club)

The Cleek was a derivative from this and was the club favoured by Allan Robertson in the 1850's. It seems he was one of the first to use the cleek regularly and not just as a "trouble shooter." Another "iron man" was young Tom Morris who began to use the Rutter to throw high balls into the green.

A third iron about this time was the Lofting Iron which was developed for shots out of sand and longer lofted shots and filled the gap between the Rutter and the Cleek.

The Rutter, the Lofting Iron and the Cleek are the Holy Trinity of iron clubs from which all the other irons developed.

THE CLUBMAKERS

In the 17th and 18th centuries one or two club makers living in St. Andrews are mentioned but the first to establish a national name was Hugh Philp (1782-1856). Originally a woodworker, he was drawn into club making when he was involved in repairing clubs. Broken shafts and split heads must have been common considering the rough ground over which golf was played.

By 1819 he became clubmaker to the Society of St. Andrews Golfers which later became the Royal and Ancient Club in 1834. Hugh Philp's gruff manner concealed a sharp wit - anyone coming to him with a complaint about one of his clubs was stopped in his tracks with the comment "Ye'll hae lost yer match?"

Tom Morris, Allan Robertson, Long Willie (Allan's helper) and Hugh Philp often had friendly games but Hugh Philp was a social, not a competitive, player and on occasion was the subject of Lang Willie's banter.

Balfour says of him "Of club-makers, no man has ever approached Hugh Philp and even now to posses a club of his is a treasure like an old Cremona violin to a musician, or a Toledo blade to a swordsman."

Robert Forgan, his nephew, joined him in 1852 and took over the business on his uncle's death four years later. Presumably this is the same Robert Forgan listed as winning our Club's 1854 January Medal with a score of 124. Robert Forgan was appointed club maker to the Prince of Wales in 1864. Thereafter the Forgan woods bore the Prince of Wales' three feathers as a trade mark.

Thanks to hard work and imagination the Forgan business prospered. Robert is given the credit of first using hickory for golf shafts. Later in the century, around 1887, the firm produced the new bulger woods and iron heads made from bronze to stop them rusting. About the end of the century the firm was employing around 40 people. By 1963, when it was bought out and closed ruthlessly, the Forgan company had trebled this number.

Another well known club making name in the town was that of Auchterlonie. By the end of the century the firm D. & W. Auchterlonie had a work force of 16 but by the 1930's it was forced to close.

There were various other small club making concerns in the town, e.g. Tom Morris and the Strath family were directly involved in club manufacture. Throughout the town various blacksmiths hammered away at hand forging the iron heads which became increasingly in demand as the years went on and the variety of irons enlarged.

Forgans 1950's

OUR CHAMPIONS

The list of champion golfers linked with St. Andrews Golf Club through the second half of last century is a formidable one. Between 1860 when the Open Championship was first played at Prestwick and 1902, twenty titles went to players associated with this club.

The only great name missing from our Open Championship Roll of Honour is Allan Robertson - probably one of the best of them all and this only because, sadly, he died the year before the Championship was first organised.

Allan Robertson was a golfing giant of his day and his involvement in the first crucial years of this Club helped to set it off on its one hundred and fifty years. In an informal competition for caddies run after the R&A's 1842 Autumn Meeting Allan was barred from competing on the insistence of the other players.

Soon after the Club's formation Allan Robertson joined us and immediately became a central figure. Early on in the Club's history he and Tom Morris were involved in the problem of organising members' "odds" or handicaps.

As Captain, in 1854, while not competing, he played in our Medals and took part in our Balls in the Town Hall with enthusiasm.

Balfour describes the "prince of golfers" in this way: "He was a short, little active man with a pleasant face, small features and a merry twinkle in his eye. He was universally popular, not a bit forward, but withal easy and full of self respect..... His style was neat and effective. He held his clubs near the end of the handle, even his putter high up. His clubs were light and his stroke an easy, swift switch. With him the game was one as much of head as of hand. He always kept cool and generally pulled through a match even when he got behind. He was a natural gentlemen, honourable and true."

A feature of golf last century was the challenge matches between the leading professionals of the day often played for large stakes with heavy betting before and even during the games. In the 1840's Allan Robertson and Tom Morris were a formidable team and on occasion were called on to play Willie and Jamie Dunn based at Musselburgh.

A famous three-cornered match took place in 1849 between them. The Dunns won easily at home, the St. Andrews pair won narrowly on the Old Course and the decider was at North Berwick. A witness of this said "I never saw a match where such vehement party spirit was displayed. So great was the keenness and the anxiety to see whose ball had the best lie, that no sooner were the shots played than off the whole crowd ran, helter skelter."

The Dunns started very strongly and built up a four hole lead in the morning, with Allan Robertson struggling. However, with two holes to go the game was squared, the Dunns hit trouble and lost by two holes.

A spectator had said to Tom Morris, when the match looked lost,

"Tom, you're going to be beaten."

Tom replied "I'm not so sure of that. The Dunnies are playing a game nae man can beat, an' they may fa' off, but there's nae fear of Allan and me fa'in off." And so it turned out.

At that time the Musselburgh course had seven holes. To make up a 36 hole match they played round five times with one extra hole. They must have been giddy at the end of it all!

A witness of this match made this comment on Allan Robertson. "Of the lot I would place Allan as the least powerful, but the most scientific. He could not play

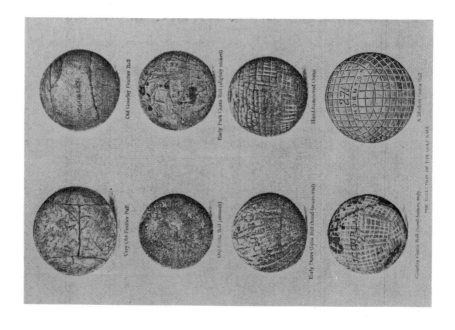

20

well on a rough green for he used light clubs and balls, and a rough grassy green was too much for him; but on St. Andrews with its unapproachable turf, he was unrivalled."

Tom Morris was six years younger than Allan Robertson and worked for him as a golf ball maker. His elder brother George was a founder member of the club and apart from young Tom, his other son, J.O.F. Morris, was a prominent club member who figures regularly in the club's records.

Tom Morris fought many battles with Willie Park. The behaviour of the crowds left a lot to be desired. In one match against Willie Park at Musselburgh a contemporary report says "Tom was roughly jostled and his ball frequently interfered with. He appealed to the referee who stopped play and declared the stakes divided."

The two first met at St. Andrews in a challenge match in 1845 and had their last encounter in 1882 at North Berwick. A writer of the time wrote "Tom Morris I need hardly describe. Who has ever handled a club and does not know him - his general countenance, dark penetrating eye, which never failed to detect a cunning road to the hole, imperturbable temper, unflinching courage and indomitable self control, under circumstances the most exasperating."

If there was one weakness in his game it was his putting. Young Tom, his son, said of his father - "If the hole was a yard nearer him, my father would be a good putter."

In 1851, Tom Morris had left the town to take up the job of greenkeeper at Prestwick but returned to St. Andrews at the invitation of the R&A as "Conservator of the Links" in 1863 and continued in the post for forty years. He died in 1908, aged 86. Tom Morris was truly a grand old man, well loved and respected both as a golfer and a person.

Young Tom in his day was outstanding. He played in his first Open at the age of 14 in 1865 and retired after 24 holes - but still one stroke better than his father.

Balfour records "'Young Tommy' was perhaps the best player that every appeared on the green. He was a tall handsome athlete and unmatched at all parts of the game. His victorious career began in 1867 when he was sixteen. It continued without a break till his early death in 1875. During these eight years he exhibited as remarkable a display of golf as has every been seen."

Another Victorian commentator had this to say - "Tommy was the embodiment of masterful energy. Every muscle of his well knit frame seemed summoned into service. He stood well back from the ball and with dashing, pressing, forceful style of driving, which seldom failed, sent it whizzing on its far and sure flight. If he chanced to top his tee, the second stroke would be an extra press of which the ball almost invariably got the full benefit.

A close friend said "His sweeping swing was magnificent. He hit the ball with

Captain Stuart

The Castle
Nottingham.
12/7/94.

Dear Sir

a friend of mine near Nottingham, wishes to make a golf link in his park. Could you kindly tell me where it would be possible to get a professional to lay it out – make the holes, etc, & could you recommend one. Also what would be the fee?

I am
Yours truly
R. Hilhouse Stuart Capt
adjt
Robin Hood Rifles

To the Secretary
St Andrew's Golf Club
N. B.

From

TOM MORRIS,

Golf Club and Ball Manufacturer,

ST ANDREWS.

15 March 1884.

To Chas. B. Grace Esq
St Andrews

Dear Sir

Your note to hand. My fee for laying out a green is £1 per day and travelling expenses.

Your obedient Servant
For Tom Morris

22

every bit of power at his command. Indeed so very hard did he hit it that at many of his long shots his Balmoral bonnet with the pheasant's claw fell off. Apart from his power he also had a deadly ability pitching and putting."

The sad end for young Tom Morris has often been told. In September 1875, while playing with his father at North Berwick against Mungo and Willie Park, word came that his wife was dangerously ill. A local resident took them across the Forth to St. Andrews in his yacht but his young wife and baby had died in childbirth. Young Tom died on Christmas day that same year. He was only 24.

There is little doubt that, had he been given his father's lifespan, he would have dominated the game for years.

Andrew Strath

How many more times would he have won the Open Championship? Speculation is entertaining but empty.

David Strath was his close companion and golfing rival. In the 1872 Open he had come second to Young Tom Morris but his name was not to appear on our Champions' Board. In 1876 he tied for first place with Bob Martin but at the 17th hole played into the green while the game in front was still on it. The ball struck a spectator and it was claimed that Strath should be disqualified. Pending a ruling the R&A ordered a play off for the next day. Strath declined to take part and Bob Martin had a walkover win.

Had he won, it would have been the second time "Strath" had appeared on the list of Open winners - his older brother Andrew having won in 1865. Both brothers were club makers in the town and both died young from consumption despite their efforts to restore their health in Australia.

The first twelve Opens were played at Prestwick and only in 1873 did it come to St. Andrews. It was appropriate that it was won by a local man, Tom Kidd. By 1872 he was well established as one of the town's finest golfers being good enough, playing with David Strath, to beat the Morrises.

This 1873 Open was also noteworthy for its high scoring (179 for two rounds) but contemporary reports indicate that there was a lot of casual water lying on the course. Tom Kidd was never able to repeat this win although he is listed in fifth place in the 1879 St. Andrews Open. He died in 1884 aged 36.

The two front runners for the 1876 Open Championship at St. Andrews were David Strath and Bob Martin, who worked as clubmakers in the town. I have described the incident resulting in Bob Martin's victory.

Tom Kidd

23

Young Tom

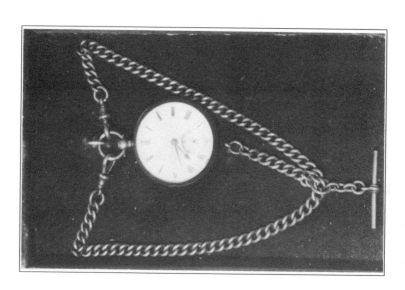

This watch, in the club's possession, was given to young Tom Morris on his 21st Birthday by his father.

Bob Martin

However, nine years later Bob Martin was to win the Open for a second time, again at St. Andrews. In the intervening years he had several times come close, notably at Prestwick in 1875 when he came second. This was the Open when Davie Ayton took third place. Bobby Burnet in his book "The St. Andrews Opens" has shown that the often repeated story of his losing the Championship through taking an eleven at the Road Hole is not true.

It was left to another St. Andrean and club member to repeat young Tom Morris's triple win in the Open. Jamie Anderson won in 1877 at Musselburgh, in 1878 at Prestwick and in 1879 on the Old Course. Some people are born winners, some born losers.

At Prestwick, Jamie Anderson produced a Houdini finish over the last four holes, including a hole in one, to edge out Bob Kirk who finished in the first five in six Opens but was another town golfer who never held the Championship Cup. In third place was J.O.F. Morris, youngest son of Tom Morris, yet another highly talented golfer who never won an Open. It was J.O.F. Morris who took part in the moonlight match against three other club members in 1887.

Jamie Anderson

In the 1870's the name Willie Fernie appeared regularly on our prize lists and, not surprisingly, he turned professional and immediately won the Open at Musselburgh in 1883. To beat Bob Ferguson, already a triple winner, on his home ground in a spectacular play off was an outstanding effort. Surprisingly it was Willie's Fernie's only win in the Championship. Between 1882 and 1899 he was in the first six on ten occasions, including three second places. Willie Fernie was one of our professionals, like several others, who kept up his association with the St. Andrews Golf Club after leaving the town. An 1887 Minute records him donating a prize for competition among our members. (The same Minute mentions the gift of a clock by Sandy Herd.)

Bob Martin had his second Open win in 1885 on his home course. Three years later another St. Andrean won, again at home. Jack Burns was a Club member who achieved fame (or notoriety) in the Club Minutes as is recorded elsewhere.

Hugh Kirkaldy won the 1891 Open in a record 166 strokes in thoroughly unpleasant conditions. A newspaper reported that he was over the road at the 18th hole into the wind and this with the old gutta ball. Universally popular, he was another of

Anderson's Medal 1878

the great names of the last century who died tragically young.

In second place was his older brother Andrew, another fine golfer who never got his name on the trophy. Andrew became a legendary figure, crusty and sharp tongued. His portrait hangs in the Club. He became an Honorary Member in 1890.

Two years later, in 1893, Willie Auchterlonie brought the Cup back to St. Andrews from Prestwick. This time the Open was played over four rounds instead of two. The seven clubs in the winner's bag were his own make and led to him setting up his own club making business in the town with his brother David in 1894.

HUGH KIRKALDY O·C· 1891

Willie Auchterlonie's name is in the Record Books for two reasons. After young Tom Morris, he was the Open's youngest winner, and he was the first to be outright leader in all four rounds. His brother Laurie was the last St. Andrean to win the American Open in 1902.

By the end of the century the firm D & W Auchterlonie was prospering. Three years later he was made an Honorary Member and maintained his contacts with the St. Andrews Golf Club until his death in 1963, aged 81.

His son Laurie took over the family shop and established a reputation as an expert on the subject of antique clubs which resulted in him being asked to help set up one of America's leading golf museums at Foxburg. When the shop was sold, his bench and some of its tools were acquired for display in the new British Golf Museum here in St. Andrews.

As the century closed club members recorded national wins abroad also. Foulis won the American Open in 1895, and in 1898 Finlay S. Douglas, who had been a student at St. Andrews University, took the American Amateur title while Fred Herd, a member of our winning team against Forfarshire the year before, won the American Open. Another member of that team, L. Auchterlonie, captured the U.S. Open in 1902 - the first man to score under 80 in all four rounds.

W. Auchterlonie

But by the year 1900 the rest of the golfing world was beginning to catch up with us. As a Club we still had some splendid wins to come but the glory days were over.

James Robb, a notable amateur, won the British Amateur Championship at Prestwick in 1906 having twice reached the final before this.

John Caven was beaten in the 1922 final of the same competition and completed an outstanding year for himself and the Club by being a member of the first ever Walker Cup team. The clubs he used are in the possession of the St. Andrews Golf Club.

In 1932 Ian McDonald won the British Boys' title. An article in the Glasgow Herald of September 1932, giving details of his victory, goes on to talk about the history of the St. Andrews Golf Club.

Among the list of Club members who won the Open it includes the name of J. Braid and his five Championships. It is known that James Braid, aged nineteen, came to St. Andrews in 1889 to work as a joiner and played with Hugh and Andrew Kirkaldy among other top golfers in the town. He moved on to Edinburgh in 1891. We know he played with our members, but did he join our club?

While Braid was serving his time as a joiner, Sandy Herd, who had become a member of our Committee, was finishing his time as a plasterer. The two became firm friends and golf partners but only in later years in England. It was 1902 before Sandy Herd won his only Open at Hoylake. The same Glasgow Herald account mentions the wins of Laurie Auchterlonie, Fred Mackenzie, Laurie Ayton, and Dennis Kyle in the "Telegraph" Cup which was the pre-runner of The Scottish Amateur Championship.

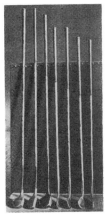

Set of clubs belonging to Willie Auchterlonie, British Open Champion 1893. Driver, brassey-niblick, midspoon, cleek, iron, mashie, and putting cleek.

Since the Second World War club members have won a variety of national trophies. George Wills' name has appeared on two - in 1955 he won the Scottish Boys' and in 1957 he won the British Youths'.

The year 1960 saw a notable double in the Scottish Boys' Championship. L. Carver

James Braid

beat S. Wilson in the final. Both were club members, the first time one club had provided both finalists.

In 1963 A. Soutar won the British Boys', and six years later Scott McDonald won the first Scottish Amateur Stroke Play Championship.

Our Club's Championship Roll of Honour starts with one of the greatest names in golf - Tom Morris. Fittingly it ends, for the moment, with another of the great names in golf - Jack Nicklaus. As is told elsewhere in the book the Club made Jack Nicklaus an Honorary Member after finishing his second round in the 1978 Open. Two days later, he came from behind and achieved the second of his St. Andrews wins. This was followed, in 1978, by his winning the Australian Open and in 1980 the American Open. If our Honorary Member can produce another Open win, we still have space on our nearly filled board for the name "J. Nicklaus."

Willie Fernie 1883

The Road Hole in the 1890's.
The only building still standing is the Station Master's house now the Jigger Inn.

Old Tom is at the window. His son, J.O.F. Morris, is in the doorway.
The second from the left is Bob Martin, twice an Open Championship winner.

Jack Burns

Andrew Kirkaldy

Sandy's Brothers - Fred Herd, U.S. Open 1898,
Brother Jim Pros. at South Shore, Chicago

Sandy Herd Open Champion 1902   *Scotland V England J. H. Taylor* Open Champion 1894-95, 1900-1913
James Braid Open Champion 1901-05-06-08-10   *1904*   *Harry Vardon* Open Champion 1896, 1898, 1899, 1903, 1911-14

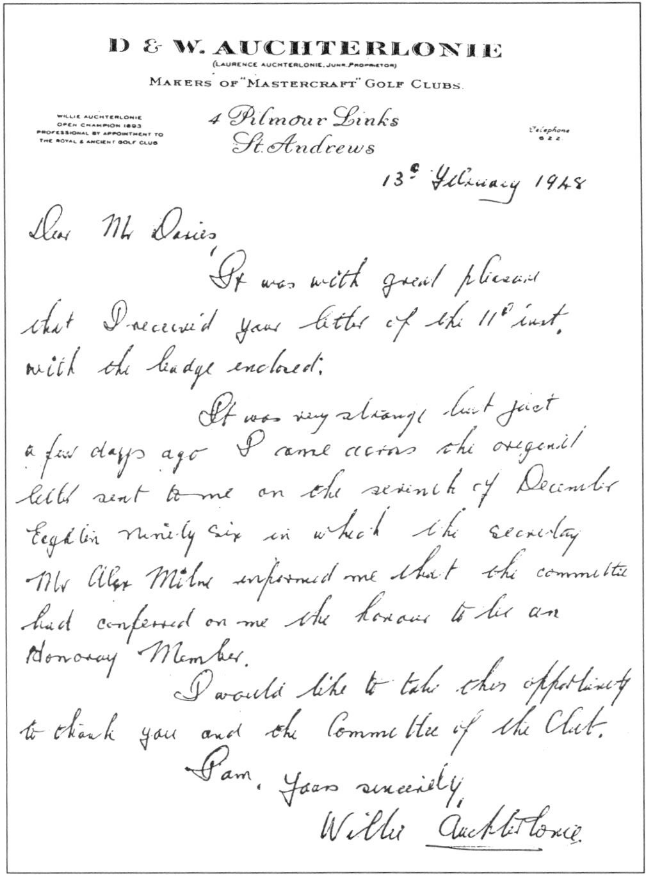

D & W. AUCHTERLONIE

(LAURENCE AUCHTERLONIE, JUNR PROPRIETOR)

MAKERS OF "MASTERCRAFT" GOLF CLUBS

WILLIE AUCHTERLONIE
OPEN CHAMPION 1893
PROFESSIONAL BY APPOINTMENT TO
THE ROYAL & ANCIENT GOLF CLUB

Telephone
622

4 Pilmour Links
St.Andrews

13th February 1948

Dear Mr Davis,

It was with great pleasure
that I received your letter of the 11th inst.
with the badge enclosed.

It was very always but just
a few days ago I came across the original
bill sent to me on the seventh of December
1946 in which the secretary
Mr Alex Milne informed me that the committee
had conferred on me the honour to be an
Honorary Member.

I would like to take this opportunity
to thank you and the committee of the Club.

I am, Yours sincerely,
Willie Auchterlonie

James Robb
Amateur Championship 1906

Alex Soutar
British Boys Championship 1963

G. Will
British Youths Championship 1957
Ryder Cup 1967
World Cup (Canada Cup) Team 1963

Ian S. McDonald
Boys Amateur Championship 1932

April 21st 1960

St Andrews Golf Club

Dear Mr President (Im sorry)

I don't remember your name, but still anyway, I won't sign to know. Still remember most of them. Im enclosing approximately 7 to 9 for you and for the boys, this slip for land for you to make all the jackets. I take you will have a real good time. Give all the Boys my Best regards and wishing you all have a good time.

I remain, Sincerely

Jock Hutchison

Jock Hutchison, born in St. Andrews, won the Open here in 1921 while a professional in America. In the first round he had a hole in one at the 8th and nearly holed his tee shot at the 9th. His three shots for two Championship holes is unequalled.

33

St ANDREWS GOLF CLUB

INSTITUTED·1843

WINNERS OF NATIONAL CHAMPIONSHIPS.

Year	Winner	Championship
1861	TOM MORRIS.	The Open
1862	TOM MORRIS.	....
1864	TOM MORRIS.	....
1865	ALEX. STRATH.	....
1867	TOM MORRIS.	....
1868	TOM MORRIS, Junr.	....
1869	TOM MORRIS, Junr.	....
1870	TOM MORRIS, Junr.	....
1872	TOM MORRIS, Junr.	....
1873	TOM KIDD.	....
1876	BOB MARTIN.	....
1877	JAMIE ANDERSON.	....
1878	JAMIE ANDERSON.	....
1879	JAMIE ANDERSON.	....
1883	WILLIE FERNIE.	....
1885	BOB MARTIN.	....
1888	JACK BURNS.	....
1891	HUGH KIRKALDY.	....
1893	W. AUCHTERLONIE.	....
1896	P. C. ANDERSON.	Amateur
1896	J. FOULIS.	American Open
1898	FRED HERD.	Do.

Year	Winner	Championship
1898	FINLAY S. DOUGLAS.	American Amateur
1902	ALEX HERD.	The Open
1902	L. AUCHTERLONIE.	American Open
1903	L B WATERS.	S. African Open
1904	L B WATERS.	Do.
1906	JAMES ROBB.	Amateur
1907	L B WATERS.	S. African Open
1920	L. B. WATERS.	Do.
1921	JOCK HUTCHISON.	The Open
1930	KEN GREIG.	Scottish Amateur
1932	IAN S. MACDONALD.	British Boys' Amateur
1946	W. R. HOPE. (M.B.·Ch.B)	Dutch Amateur
1955	GEORGE WILL.	Scottish Boys'
1957	GEORGE WILL.	British Youths'
1960	LACHLAN CARVER.	Scottish Boys'
1963	ALEX H.C. SOUTAR.	British Boys' Amateur
1969	J. SCOTT MACDONALD.	Scot Open Amateur Stroke Play
1978	JACK NICKLAUS.	The Open
1978	JACK NICKLAUS.	Australian Open
1980	JACK NICKLAUS.	American Open

JUST A MINUTE (I)
(1843 - 1893)

Any golf club historian's first task is to read through the Minutes and gey dreich work it can be. There are times when the Minutes seem like Hours! There is a lot of dross to be sifted through. The spelling, punctuation and grammar can be erratic and the writing often ranges from the adequate to the near unreadable. No sooner have you mastered one secretary's script than he resigns and you have to get to grips with his successor's. I heaved a sigh of relief when I came to the first typed Minutes in 1972.

Our first Minute Book has disappeared without trace. Its absence is recorded as early as 1938. However, James Sorley wrote a series of weekly articles on the history of the Club in the St. Andrews Citizen commencing 14th February 1911. In his introduction he says "I have luckily come across the Minutes of the Club since its birth right on to the year 1860."

The loss of the Club's second Minute Book from 1860 to 1883 is recorded thus:
Golf Inn, April 10th 1886

"The Capt. moved that Sec. write to W. Brown, late Sec. for Old Minute Book, Sec. A. Bell who stated that he had sent it to him when he (A. Bell) retired from office."

Golf Inn, June 1st 1886

"The Capt. stated that he was informed that he had given the late Secy, liberty to destroy the old Minute Book which he denied as it was not in his power to do so."

Fortunately Robert Baptie produced a series of articles on the history of the Club in 1933 and partially filled the gap from 1860 to 1883 by going back through copies of the "Fife Herald" and "St. Andrews Citizen". Thanks to both, we do have the St. Andrews Golf Club's first Minute recorded.

"At St. Andrews the 29th September 1843 a number of young men met to consider what steps should be taken to form themselves into a Society when it was proposed and agreed to that this Society should be considered as instituted on this day and be called the St. Andrews Mechanics' Golf Club when it was proposed by A. Carstairs, cabinet maker, and seconded and unanimously agreed to that D. Todd, jun., painter, should be made Captain of the Club for the first year."

Signed DAVID TODD

In the centenary history A.J. Bennett gives the names of our eleven founder members. They deserve an honourable mention. They were William Ayton, Cabinet maker; Alexander Carstairs, Cabinet maker; Alexander Bruce, Cabinet maker; James Herd, Mason; John Keddie, Joiner; John Lynn, Tailor; Adam McPherson, Plasterer; James McPherson, Dancing Master; George Morris, Butler; Robert Paterson, Slater; and David Todd, Junior, Painter.

From the occupations recorded it is obvious that the word "Mechanic" as used in 1843 covered all kinds of skilled trades and did not have the narrow meaning we now give it.

The details of our first A.G.M. are brief:

"At St. Andrews, the 30th September 1844, the annual meeting of the Club it was proposed by the retiring Chairman that Robert Wilson, blacksmith, should be Captain of the Club, which was agreed to, upon which he begged leave to decline the honour and made an amendment that the present Chairman be re-elected for another year, which, after considerable discussion and uproar was agreed to on the understanding that that rule should not be gone into in the future."

Signed DAVID TODD

By the third annual meeting on 25th September 1846 our members were firming up the Club's organisation saying "That owing to the increase of members and the thriving state at which it had arrived, a minute book be kept entirely for the Club to govern them" and "that D. Todd should be elected secretary and treasurer jointly which office he accepted and got orders to buy a book before the next meeting."

A Committee was appointed made up of the Chairman, Croupier (a kind of M.C.), Treasurer and Secretary, and one other member which at its first meeting agreed "that the Committee be empowered to lift the money then gathered and order a medal for the Club to be played for over the links of St. Andrews only and that the Treasurer be always in the possession of the said medal except on meetings of the club at any time at the discretion of the Committee."

Following on the "uproar" of our 1844 annual meeting we then had a lively first meeting of the Committee which fell out badly about the arrangement for the new Medal competition.

DAVID TODD, First Captain, 1843

The first motion was passed without controversy - "D. Todd moved that players of the medal should be members of the club for at least one calendar month" but "John Lynn, tailor, then moved that Richard Litster be appointed Secretary and was seconded by A. McPherson which was agreed to, upon which D. Todd tendered his resignation to take effect at next meeting of the Club."

Feathers were unruffled on 20th December 1846 when Allan Robertson proposed that "D. Todd's resignation as Secretary and Treasurer should not be accepted of at present but that he should act as he has heretofore done" and this was agreed to. He also proposed "That the medal be played for over the Links twice a year."

Our first formal competition on January 1st 1847 was recorded "At St. Andrews Links the medal was played for and was won by James Herd at 105 strokes and the prize given by Allan Robertson was won by Wm. Ayton, jun. at 111 strokes." That first medal is now part of the Captain's Chain of Office.

At a meeting on 19th June the following rules were agreed to:

1. That the next senior member of the Club be the succeeding Chairman, if at the annual meeting in September.

2. That the Secretary and Treasurer conjunctly be elected annually in September.

3. That the members meet quarterly and each pay threepence per quarter to keep a standing sum for incidental expenses.

4. Individuals wishing to become members must give in a written application of their intention to the Chairman, with at least two members assigned to said application. Entry money 2/-.

5. That all members be elected by, and only when a majority of members are in their favour, at a special meeting called for such purpose, and the person or persons to be elected to be entered only by vote by ballot. Nine to form a quorum.

6. That in the event of any disagreement among the members, the funds and property to belong to those members who adhere to the rules preceding this at the time of such disagreement.

7. That if any member allows himself to be in arrears more than one year, he shall be held not a member until he pay 1/- over and above one year's payments.

8. That the foregoing rules cannot be altered but by a majority of two-thirds of the members at a special meeting for such purpose.

By the following April these had been extended as follows:-

1st. That the entry money be raised to 3s.

2nd. That every individual applying for admission to the Club must be proposed at one meeting and balloted for at another.

3rd. That the conduct of ....on the first day of the year be taken into consideration.

4th. That the conduct of ....on the first night of the year be apologised for by him.

5th. That all the prizes intending to be given to the Club to be played for at the half-yearly meetings be intimated to the Committee two weeks before the day of competition and that no prize be accepted after that date."

We can allow ourselves a quiet smile at Item 3 and 4. The first full years of the Club's life had already seen a stormy first annual meeting, an equally fiery first Committee Meeting and now two members warned as to their future conduct!

There was worse to come -

29th September 1848

"At the annual meeting of this date the following office-bearers were elected according to rule 1. Alex Bruce, cabinet-maker, was called to the chair; David Thomson was called upon to be Croupier, Adam McPherson Committee member, and David Todd was elected for the office of treasurer and secretary as heretofore. Then the Club sat down to supper at Mr. Ritchie's City Hotel when a disturbance arose which ended the meeting in uproar and confusion."

(Signed) ALEX BRUCE

However "Three days later, on the 2nd October, a special meeting was called at the requisition of nine members 'To take into consideration the conduct of several of the members at their last meeting'. It was moved, seconded, and unanimously agreed to that an apology be taken from .... and another, and it was also unanimously agreed to that in consequence of the conduct of ....he be dismissed from the Club and to have no right or title to any of the funds or property now or may be belonging to this Club."

The two members required to apologise were prominent Committee members! Thus ended the Club's first supper. Reading between the lines it might well have been our last supper!

By this time all kinds of interesting suggestions were being made. For example, in 1847 a red Club jacket was proposed but this did not seem to come to anything. At the meeting of 25th September 1848 it was agreed to hold a Club Ball and look into the possibility of a Club flag.

Our first match with Leven was first proposed at a Club meeting on 18th October 1849. The following letter was sent:

"Gentlemen, - I am requested by the St. Andrews Mechanics Golf Club to invite you to a friendly game of golf, and shall be glad to hear from you upon the subject. In the event of your agreeing, we would say that you state the number of players you would place against an equal number of ours - not less than six nor more than twelve - and that the first heat come off on your Links, and the next on ours, and as we can expect to have a meeting on Friday first, we would like to have an answer from you to lay before said meeting. By doing so you will oblige. -

Yours with respect (signed) D. Todd."

Robert Baptie gives us the details of the resultant home and away games.

"The Leven golfers evidently had been ready for the fray, as within three weeks from the date of the meeting the match had been played. The Club paid to each player a sum of 2s. as a contribution towards their expenses at the match, which took place at Leven on 1st November. Thus began a series of games which although broken for a number of years, continues to the present time. It may interest members to know that this match was first played on a Thursday."

"Six members represented each Club, but about 20 went down to Leven. Unfortunately, the names of the players are not known, but neither Allan Robertson nor Tom Morris was in the team, as the Club thought they were strong enough without the assistance of the two 'cracks'. It was a great day for St. Andrews, who won by 19 holes to 2, and the social gathering which followed was a fitting finish to the auspicious occasion. It was bright moonlight when the team left Leven, and the journey soon passed, but the victors were hardly prepared for the welcome they got when they reached home. Practically every member who had stayed at home waited for them, besides many others, who gave the triumphant golfers a right royal welcome.

Our team v Leven 1886
Did any losers get horse whipped?

The return match was played on St. Andrews Day, 30th November, at St. Andrews and, as was to be expected, resulted in another triumph for St. Andrews. The same players took part, and the result was a victory for St. Andrews by 34 holes. The Leven party numbered nineteen, and in the evening a company of forty sat down to supper in the City Hotel. David Thomson, the Captain, presided over the gathering, and after the cloth had been cleared, the evening was spent in toast and song, and although the Leven players went home defeated, they were a contented crowd, as friendships had been made which proved lasting."

Handicapping was becoming a lively issue. James Sorley's own observations written in 1911 deserve quoting:

"In golf just like any other game, there are outstanding players or plus men, good average players or scratch men, fair players or those with a moderately low handicap, and lastly 'duffers' with huge handicaps - generating the limit. The latter toil laboriously in a hopeless endeavour to master the intricacies of the game, and spend much time and energy in so doing, but all in vain. Your average 18 handicap player may bring himself down to the 14 handicap mark, but there he remains for the rest of his golfing days.

Of course, there are exceptions, but I am speaking generally. However, the 'duffer' is, as a rule, nothing if not an optimistic and cheerful soul, and seems to get as much pleasure out of the game as your scratch or plus men do, and in every Club he forms a goodly percentage of the membership. He is a useful member, too, and generally to be found on the Committee. Again he is good for trade. Therefore, he must be treated with due consideration, hence the system of handicapping which prevails in all Clubs."

AMEN

Allan Robertson sent this letter to our Committee arguing against individual handicaps:-

Links, St. Andrews,

Dec. 20th 1849

"Sir, - According to my statement in last meeting, I move that no odds be given to the players for either medal or other prizes, but that all members of the Club should be classed into one, two, three, four or five classes, also that a prize be given to each class and the medal open to all the members, this motion to take effect on and after January 1st 1850."

I am, Sir, yours truly,

(Signed) ALLAN ROBERTSON

To the Members of the Mechanics Golf Club

This was accepted and it was arranged that the Committee meet with him and Tom

Morris to classify our players into groups.

In June 1850 it was decided to order two cross clubs of silver at a cost not exceeding two pounds to provide a prize for another annual competition.

This, our second oldest trophy, is currently the first handicap prize in our Spring Meeting. Under the heading "Changed Days Nowadays" James Sorley has this comment on the two club prizes:-

"In 1850 all they had to compete for were the medal and cross clubs with the addition perhaps of a couple of golf balls or a golf club presented by a member, and the Club was very thankful for any little gift of a prize to swell the meagre list on medal days. Now we have at least a dozen prizes - more, to be correct, with the addition of corresponding sweepstakes.

I wonder what sort of an entry we would have on medal days, should the prizes at stake be only the medal, cross clubs (both merely held by the winner for six months), a couple of golf balls and a club and no sweepstake? I am afraid there would be no entries at all. But they were not pot-hunters in the olden days, and played for the glory and love of the game. Not many of us do so now."

A meeting was held in Mr. Hastie's Inn at which it was decided that handicapping of individual players be re-introduced. Other Rules were drawn up including:-

"VIII.- That for the due preservation of order at meetings of this Club every member who has anything to say shall rise and address the Chair in respectful language; upon no account is any improper or unbecoming language to be used or personalities indulged in; any member guilty of such conduct to be called to order by the Chairman, and upon repetition of the offence to be ordered to quit the room, and not be suffered to enter until sufficient apology has been handed in.

IX. Should any rupture occur and in consequence the partial dismemberment of the Club result, all books, paper, monies, and other Club property to be recognised as belonging to those remaining members - who agree to abide by and adhere to the rules and regulations."

Again, Allan Robertson and Tom Morris were called in to arrange handicaps. The former suggested "that no member be made aware of his odds until his return from playing." It was also decided at this last meeting of the year that the Club discontinue booking a Band to play them up from the Links after the New Year's Day Competition. The practice of firing a gun at the start and finish of the competition was a part of the day's ceremonial retained. It is recorded that the powder cost around 1/-. The Minute goes on:-

"It was agreed to meet in Mr. Ritchie's house (City Hotel) at half-past nine a.m. on the morning of the 'medal' for the purpose of making preliminary arrangements, also, that the competitions start at 10 o'clock, the order of starting to be by ballot, and that no matches be entered upon until all the competitors are in. The members agreed to dine together as formerly in the evening in Mr. Hastie's Inn; dinner to be on the table at 5 o'oclock. On the motion of James Howie, the Club unanimously agreed to walk the marches on the second day of January along with the Town Council should that body agree to do so."

Once again James Sorley's own comments are worth including because they provide illumination on golfing affairs around 1911.

"THE WALKING THE MARCHES

was an assertion of their claim or right to play over the Links, which in those days belonged to the town, and every player had equal privileges. Of course, I am aware that the Links still belong to the town, although sometimes one is apt to think differently judging from the year in, year out agitation which takes place between our Town Council and the Royal and Ancient Golf Club, neither party being able to come to a suitable agreement. Our golf links nowadays can be likened unto a bone over which two dogs are fighting. Each has got an end of it, and neither will let go. Arbitration steps in in the person of a passer-by who separates the contestants. St. Andrews people are still wondering when and how the 'bone of contention' will be settled."

The Old Town Tolbooth stood in the middle of Market Street opposite the Cross Keys Hotel

At the half-yearly meeting on Friday, 27th June 1851 it was decided to hold the Club's first Ball. After a lengthy discussion it was agreed:-

James Howie

"1st. That the ticket include nothing out of the ball-room, and that all parties pay additionally for what refreshments they may choose.

2nd. That one pound be allocated from the funds towards the expenses, and all members to have free tickets admitting themselves and three partners, if they please, any further sum in name of expenses to be made up by those members of the Club who were present at the ball.

3rd. That a stranger or non-member be admitted on approval of the Committee, upon payment of one shilling and sixpence for a single ticket, and two shillings for double ticket admitting three partners.

4th. That it shall be optional with all parties whether or not they shall take supper, but in an hour set apart when those inclined to have refreshments shall lift together for that purpose."

A meeting of the whole Club on 9th September established that twenty members were prepared to attend and guarantee any loss. The final arrangements stated "The liquors to be supplied by Mr. Hastie of the Cross Keys and the refreshments by Mr. Mackenzie, confectioner, on the understanding that they pay the hall expenses. Mr. James McPherson was to be asked if he could furnish the necessary music, viz. violin, violincello, and flute and at what cost and in the event of Mr. McPherson declining or circumstances arising to interfere or prevent such an arrangement to engage Mr. Peter Sharpe." Our first Ball made a profit of 2s.8d.

Every golf club requires leaders who are prepared to look imaginatively at the future, produce new ideas and provide the drive to get them implemented. One such was James Howie who argued strongly for a simplification of the Club's name and urged the need for a Clubhouse.

About the Club's title he suggested:-

"Let the present limited name be exchanged for a more enlarged one. Instead of calling it 'The Mechanics Golf Club' let it be called 'the St. Andrews Golf Club' or some such comprehensive title. The result of such an alteration would be the admission into our Club of a vast number of tradesmen and shopkeepers, which would tend to elevate us and it would also put us on a level of respectability with other Golf Clubs, and we would then appear alongside of them in the Fife list and Edinburgh Almanack."

James Hastie appreciated the value to any golf club of having its own premises and urged the members:-

"That they take steps to ascertain the practicability of obtaining premises to suit the purpose of Union Parlour where the Club meeting could be held, the clubs and playing dress of members be kept, etc. The advantages of such a place for the members of our Club either in point of comfort, convenience, or economy, are scarcely to be calculated, and the result of having such a place would be to place us in a position that it would soon be a matter of some importance to become a member of the St. Andrews Golf Club."

How right he was!

In 1847 the decision to have a Club flag had been taken but it was five years before it appeared.

At a special meeting of the Club held on 23rd January 1852, in the Town Hall, we are told "a considerable number of the members, accompanied by their wives and friends being present - the Captain presiding - the Captain stated the object of the meeting, which was in honour of the ladies for giving the Club the flag, and after some fitting remarks he begged to propose a toast to the ladies, which the Secretary, David Thomson, replied to in name of the ladies present, and then handed the flag over to the care of the Captain. After a most agreeable night of harmony the meeting broke up."

The flag measured nine feet by six feet and on a white ground, there were put corners consisting of a Union Jack, a Scotch Thistle, the Lion Rampant, and St. Andrew supporting the Cross. In the centre were crossed clubs and balls in blue. Thereafter it would be flown on medal days outside the Golf Inn which seems to have been on the site of the Links Hotel.

The third Annual Ball ran into problems and it was necessary to go round the members personally to get the required number of signatures. Three musicians were engaged for 7/- each "inclusive of refreshments". There seemed to have been some friction with the caterer's wife - "It was distinctly said to Mr. Scott's better half and understood that Mr. Scott bear the expense of gas and the cleaning up of the upper hall." The report on the Ball reads:

"On the 21st of this month, October 1853, the third annual ball came off in the Town Hall. The ballroom was tastefully decorated with flowers and evergreens. The Musicians were Messrs. McPherson, Sharpe and Liddell. Nearly fifty couples were present, but owing to the Leven Club holding their Medal Day the week before, none of the members of that body were present. Dancing commenced at half-past nine o'clock; at 12 o'clock the parties retired to the Upper Hall for refreshments. After an agreeable hour, dancing was resumed at one o'clock, and owing to the hilarity and agreement was kept up till far into the morning. In every way the ball went off well helped by the ever cheerful countenance of our most worthy Captain - **Allan Robertson - the World's King of Clubs.**"

Allan Robertson

Throughout the Minutes of the Club in the 19th century are details of a wide variety of unusual donated prizes. There cannot be many clubs whose members have competed for two gold nuggets!

"St. Andrews, 10th Oct. 1854.

A special meeting was held in Mr. Hastie's in consequence of the Captain receiving two nuggets of gold from his brother in Australia to be played for round the links.

It was agreed to play for the gold on Thursday first, to start at 8 o'clock, and meet at half-past 7 o'clock in Mr. Hastie's to give some honour to Mr. David Robertson for his donation.

This competition resulted in George Morris winning first prize with a fine score of 91. The second nugget was gained by Mr. McPherson, 98 - 5 = 93.

The members met in the evening in Mr. Hastie's and did honour to Mr. David Robertson."

There were regular reports on the Club's activities in the local Press. One dated January 1851 reads:-

"'Mechanics' Golf Club - The competition for the honours took place over our links on New Year's Day. The weather was fine, and the play was remarkably good. The silver medal was gained by Mr. William Ayton, jun., at 94 strokes; the silver cross

Big Bunker in front of teeing ground to second hole, 1852

club, by Mr. George Morris, at 96 strokes. The club presented by Messrs. Robertson and Ayton was gained by William Ayton, jun., at 94. The club presented by Mr. James McPherson, by Mr. Robt. Paterson, at 96. The ball presented by Mr. Allan Robertson, gained by Mr. Alexander Grieve, at 97 - odds being allowed in competing for the four prizes. As illustrative of the state of play as intimated above, we may mention that the gold medal of the Royal and Ancient Golf Club was taken at 100 strokes. The members dined together in the evening in Mr. Hastie's Inn. Mr. Robert Paterson, captain, presided. The cheer was of Mr. Hastie's best. The greatest harmony prevailed. Toast, song, and sentiment abounded. We have reason to believe that the formation of this and another club among our working classes has been of considerable social advantage to them. A person who went round the links informed us that he counted 349 tradesmen there, very few of whom were intoxicated although it was New Year's Day."

No doubt the person quoted was able to comment equally favourably on the sobriety of our friends in the R&A who were also playing that day.

Another report dated June 1853 states:

"St. Andrews Golf Club - The half-yearly competition of this society, formerly called 'The Mechanics' Golf Club', took place on Friday afternoon, which happened to be uncommonly favourable for play, rain having fallen in the forenoon, an occurrence highly advantageous to the putting department. The best play was that of Mr. George Morris, brother of the well-known Tom, who went round the course in 93, and, consequently, got the Medal. Mr. John Lynn, tailor, was next at 96, for which he got the Silver Cross. Mr. James McPherson was third dux at 100. The prizes were won as under specified:-

Two balls, presented by		
Allan Robertson	-	Mr. Adam McPherson
Two balls, presented by		
Thomas Morris	-	Mr. Alexander Clyne, tailor
Driving Club	-	Mr. David Clark
Putter	-	Mr. Alexander Galloway
Another ball	-	Mr. Wm. Ayton, sen.
" "	-	Mr. George Bruce

All the gainers of the prizes received various odds in reckoning the scores, on account of inferiority to the standard players. There appears to be an erroneous system of arranging the odds. For instance, one prize-holder actually went round in 106, and had the immense odds of 31 to substract from that number, which brought his score to 75 - a number which it is impracticable for any man to hole the Links in, or anything near it. Allan Robertson's smallest score is 83".

Allan Robertson was made Captain in 1853. As the leading player of this time, obviously his membership of our Club in its early years gave it substantial status. All reports suggest he took his Captaincy seriously and led the Club well and enthusiastically.

A newspaper clipping from January 1854 reports:

"The Captain (Allan Robertson) with the whole members of the Mechanics' Golf Club played round the Links in a body, when Mr. Robert Forgan scored 124..." The Links were "in a very unfit state for playing from snow and ice." Regularly through 150 years of Minutes, the New Year's Day weather shows itself predictably unpredictable.

Last century the town's golfers took the game seriously but they also knew how to enjoy themselves after their rounds. None more so than our rivals in the St. Andrews Operatives' Club. Following their competition on New Year's morning, 1852:

"The members of the Operative Club dined together in the Royal Hotel. About twelve o'clock the hammers, putting-stone, leaping apparatus, skittles, etc. etc. of the Gymnastic Club were brought out, and many friendly matches took place. Towards afternoon, a very considerable number of the town's people were looking on, and then the pole climbing commenced. The pole was twice fairly climbed, and once unfairly by a person who soaked his trousers with water, and daubed them full of sand, but the trick was detected. The bell race succeeded. All the sports went off very well indeed; there were no disturbances, and scarcely a drunk person to be seen, either on the links or streets."

They showed an impressive stamina.

Some of the medal scores for 8th October 1858 are interesting:

1. George Bruce 100-5-95 Forgan's club
2. Jas McPherson 104 scr 104 Ayton's club
3. John Lynn 106 scr l05 Allan's two balls

Bringing up the rear was W. Davidson 178-25-153! No competition was complete without the prize-giving and social evening but a little piece of social history was mentioned in the Minutes in the following year:-

"What is this? 'The members after the competition sat down to supper in the Golf Inn and enjoyed themselves till Forbes McKenzie stopped their enjoyment.' The reference to Forbes McKenzie is a joke. Forbes McKenzie was the man who brought in the 11 o'clock Closing Act." - as James Sorley reminds us.

1859 saw the death of Allan Robertson at the age of 44. He had been a very popular captain and a very loyal club member as well as being one of the greatest players of his time.

The loss of the Minute Book covering 1860-83 has meant that any Club records

47

have been taken from the newspapers of the period.   The regular competitions feature. In March 1871 a new series of fortnightly medals were played between March and October for a gold charm.   "The charm, which was of gold and bore civic and golfing designs, was procured by contributions from the competitors with a special donation from G. Honeyman, Golf Hotel."

1873 saw the first match with Carnoustie.   Robert Baptie suggests it may have been talked about at an earlier match between Monifieth and the St. Andrews Rose Club, which included some of our players.   Traditionally matches were played out to the 18th green.   There were twelve in each team and it was played on a Home and Away basis.   St. Andrews won by eight holes.

The same year Thomas Reynolds, King of a Gypsy tribe from Norfolk presented a timepiece as a prize to be competed for by our players and those from the St. Andrews Rose Club. The gypsy encampment was in a field beside the Station Master's house (now the Jigger Inn).

Our captain, William Ayton, was leader of a legal dispute with the town's magistrates in 1879 over their proposal to construct what is now the road running past the front door of our Clubhouse.

In 1820 the town had feued the triangle of ground from the Swilcan Burn up to Golf Place but a condition of this was that there would be no further encroachment on Links ground.   The first houses faced on to the main road which was then the Turnpike road to Guardbridge and there were gates in their back walls which led onto the Links.

The problem arose when the owners began to build second properties on their ground facing on to the Old Course.   These were built on the edge of the feued plots but then required a road to provide access.   William Ayton and his fellow complainants argued that this infringed the original agreement made in 1820.

The case was heard in Edinburgh and all kinds of conflicting evidence was brought.   The defendants claimed that there had always been a road which had run up from Grannie Clark's Wynd and cut across what is now the 18th green to join Golf Place.

Local people gave evidence that there had been a continuous wall from Allan Robertson's house on the corner down towards the site of the R & A Clubhouse and there had not been a proper track.   By the time of the lawsuit the top part of The Links had been made into a grass terrace with seats on it.   Despite this the judge ruled that the road could be built.

However, this was not the end of the matter.   When the Town Council moved in early in 1880 to lay the new road open warfare broke out.   As the Council's workmen laid down the road metal a second squad of men hired by the opposition took it away.   Thereafter the situation became farcical.   The rebels' workmen then offered to bring the material back if the price was right.   Before the anti-road organisers realised what

A Club minute dated 17th June 1853 reads
"The Club agreed to form a group on Medal day to be taken as a photographic picture
by Mr. Rodger who kindly volunteered his services for that purpose.'
This picture shows the Club members in 1878

was happening a deal was done by the Council and both squads of men started relaying the road. That night efforts were made to destroy the road again and only a firm threat by the Chief Constable of imprisonment for anyone caught doing this finally ended the conflict. The history of St. Andrews is full of battles between developers and conservationists. On this occasion the developers won!

In 1879 there was a presentation to W. Ayton, who had been elected to the captaincy for the ninth successive year, of a pair of field glasses and a gold scarf.

William Ayton Jnr.

Every golfing calendar needs some light relief - Robert Baptie has this account of an internal club match between the Married Men and Bachelors:

"Are the married members better golfers than the single men? This question agitated the minds of the members of the Club for some time. Claims and counterclaims were advanced by both classes, and at last it was decided to put the matter to the test by playing a match between teams of married and single members. Thursday, 15th July 1880, was chosen for the match, the first match to go off at 6 o'clock. Twenty-eight members took part, fourteen on each side and, when the last match got home, it was found, on comparing the results, that the single men had won by 21 holes to 13. Adjourning to the Golf Hotel, the match was played over again, and the married men, thinking it was probably a fluke result, threw out a challenge for another match the following week.

For the second match, the teams were increased to eighteen a side, but the increased numbers did not have the expected effect, as this time the married men were overwhelmed to the extent of 35 holes to 2. This match was also fought over again in the Golf Hotel, and a Mr. T.B. Elliot handed £1 to the Captain to help to defray the expenses of the meeting after the match.

The match had created a good deal of interest among the local people, as well as among the members of the Club, and most of the games were followed by spectators. The game which aroused the most interest was one in which R. Braid and R. Anderson, representing the Benedicts, were opposed by James Fenton (the skipper) and David Corstorphine, and a large crowd followed them round.

The married men must have thought that this display in the second match was too bad to be true, for they made arrangements to play another match on Saturday, 31st July. This time it was mutually agreed to get the assistance of the professionals who were honorary members of the Club, and Bob Martin, Tom Kidd and James Anderson appeared in the married men's team, while the bachelors had the aid of J.O.F. Morris and David Ayton. The inclusion of Champion James Anderson and ex-Champions

Bob Martin and Tom Kidd gave the married men much moral support, and this match saw them in a better light, though still defeated, the margin on this occasion being 19-15 in favour of the bachelors. Again great interest was taken in the match, a big crowd following the first game, in which the contestants were Bob Martin and Tom Kidd against J.O.F. Morris and Davie Ayton, the ex-Champions winning on the last green".

There were two firsts in 1881. What seems to have been our first knock-out competition was organised. The prize was presented by R. Kirk, clubmaker and the winner was William Ayton, now Vice Captain after ten years in the captaincy. The other was our first game with Monifieth.

The Minutes resume in 1883. Apart from giving us an idea of golf last century, they provide all kinds of insights into life in the town. Wherever possible I have left the Minutes to speak for themselves.

21st Sept. 1883. "Pies as usual to be on the table at 8 o'clock. It was also agreed that the Secretary should send notice to the Royal & Ancient that we intend to commence play at half past two on Saturday afternoon."

29th Sept. 1883. "Which day the St. Andrews Golf Club held their Annual Medal Competition and in the evening had a very harmonious meeting in the Golf Hotel, Capt. Doherty in the Chair. Several songs being sung by various members of the Club, the usual loyal and Complimentary Toasts being given from the Chairman, the Company broke up about 11 o'clock after singing Auld Lang Syne."

"The following were the successful Competitors ("list lost and can't be found" - N. Brown.)"

9th May 1884. "The members met in the evening for the distribution of prizes and after which the members and their friends spent the evening with song and sentiment to the satisfaction of all present and after singing Auld Lang Syne parted in peace."

3rd Oct. 1885. "On which day the members of St. Andrews Golf Club met to play for their Medal and Prizes. 28 members were balloted. The Committee met at 7 p.m. and went over the scoring cards, 27 having been handed in.... A discussion arose in regard to 6 members who had played for the Championship, they having been classed as professionals. Before any settlement had been made, the members met, the Capt. in the chair, pies were served after which the prize list was taken up. Other 4 cards had been handed in between the time the members met and the prize list taken up belonging to D. Anderson 96, J. Auchterlonie 93, J. Burns 88, W. Greig 89, 4 of the members who had been playing for the cup. These not having been gone over, R. Braid 91 was declared medal holder which was disputed by J. Burns who said he was the winner with an 88 score. He, having lifted 30/- prize money, was classed as a professional. He denied lifting a prize. Witnesses having been brought it was proved he had. He was therefore disqualified. Burns, being out of order and insulting the Captain and another member, was expelled from the room.

Note: Owing to the uproarious state of the meeting I could not enter all that was said and done into the minutes which I hope you will excuse. I think I have most if not all the main points entered."

Oct. 15 1885. "Mr. J. Honeyman asked why he had not been instructed to order and pay for the pies as usual, the Sec. and Tres. having done so. After explaining that they were new office bearers he was satisfied. The minutes were then approved of."

"A discussion was raised by A. Gourlay anent the members who played for the cup on Oct. 3rd. W. Blair asked what they entered as. D. Honeyman said as profs. D. Anderson said when he was asked what he entered as he said a confectioner. W. Blair stated as far as he could understand they were profs. for all time coming."

"A. Milne asked if there was any precedent whereby any member was disqualified for playing in a competition and not lifting a prize. A. Gourlay stated that his brother had been disqualified for so doing. Capt. Ayton moved that minutes of com. meeting be held as null and void, sec. by A. Milne and agreed. To get the voice of the club as to whether the members who played for the cup were to be disqualified or not. D. Honeyman pro. that they be balloted, sec. by W. Blair. Jas Auchterlonie made an amendment that they take a show of hands, sec. by A. Carstairs. The motion was carried by Ballot. They were then balloted. To admit 15, reject 9. Majority to admit 6. The prizes were then distributed. Capt. Ayton said he would resign his seat as Capt. D. Honeyman requested the Secy. to withdraw his name and his brothers from the books of the club."

The question of whether Club members who were professionals should be allowed to play in our medals was obviously a divisive one. The fact that William Ayton, the captain and other club members were prepared to resign over the issue indicates that feelings ran very high. W. Ayton was captain also in the following year (1886) and this suggests that peace broke out.

Allan Robertson and Tom Morris, both professionals and both members did not play in our competitions but took part in the social life of the Club. Throughout the 19th century a series of professionals were connected with the club as members or honorary members presumably on the same basis.

In 1900 when J. Anderson, entered from the Ancient Order of Foresters Club, won the R&A Gold Medal, the runner up, a member of our club, protested that Anderson had been a professional in the U.S.A. However the R&A ruled that the competition was open to all members of St. Andrews Golf Clubs. Soon after Anderson was admitted to membership of the St. Andrews Golf Club and thereafter it seems that professionals did take part in Club competitions.

Laurie Ayton Snr., after a very distinguished professional career in the U.S.A. and Britain, came back home to St. Andrews, became Club Captain in 1953 and competed regularly in club events.

In the 50-aside match with Carnoustie it is still normal to find professional golfers

St. Andrews from the Sands

THE LINKS, ST ANDREWS.

The Links, St. Andrews

from both clubs taking part in this historic fixture which was first played in 1873, and professionals who are Club members can still play in our Club competitions.

Oct. 15th 1885

"A Bell, Tres. of Ball Comm. read the Ball report. There was a deficiency of 6/3d owing to H. Wilson, a member of B Com, having decamped with 36/- being the value of 12 tickets he had sold. The deficiency was granted from the club funds. The report was then approved. A. McRobbie moved that no proceedings be taken against Wilson at present. Secy to be instructed to try and get his address and write to him, sec by A. Black. The meeting was then closed".

Note: (Dec. 29. A. Bell stated that he had received 32/- from Wilson).

On 26th March 1886 first mention is made of Alex Herd who was to become Open Champion in 1902. He became a committee member later in the same year.

The Minutes also includes reference to a letter from Leven Thistle requesting that our Championship players should not be included in our team to play them. This was unacceptable to our Committee.

May 15th 1886

"On which day the members met for the Annual Spring competition. 30 members were balloted to start. The Committee met after all had returned and found that Jas. Fenton was 1st at 94. D. Anderson & W. Greig tied at 95. Fenton's card was disputed having from 6th to 5th hole taken 6 strokes whereas he had only 5 on his card. His marker stated that he had played 6 strokes but that his caddie (Fenton's) cried out 5 and he thought he might have miscounted. When Fenton was asked he could not mind how many he took to that hole. He was ultimately kept out of the prize list."

Golf Inn, August 25 1886.

"Capt. read a letter from Capt. Jackson, Leven Thistle G.C. anent match to be played on 28th. Johnston's offer was accepted, namely Bus with 4 in hand for 2/6 per head. Davidson's offer was £3 if you guaranteed 24. It was agreed to leave St. Andrews at 10 a.m. and Leven 7.30 p.m."

Golf Inn, Dec. 17th 1886.

"J. Robertson made a motion that the value prizes be placed on the table and that the winners choose their own beginning with the first winner, sec. by A. Lorimer. W. Ayton made an amendment that they be valued and placed according to their value, sec. by J. Pirrie. The motion was carried by vote."

Dec. 29th 1886

"On which night the Committee of St. Andrews Golf Club met to arrange prize list, Capt. Stark presiding. A. Bell moved that the committee take the books over from the collectors which was agreed to. On being examined it was found the amount collected in money £9.18.6, in value £1.9.6. J. Pirie moved that the collectors get 10 per cent, sec. by A. Milne and agreed to.   They were also allowed 6/6d for refreshments."

April 29th 1887.

"The following 7 candidates were then balloted. Thos. King, cabinet maker, pro. by A. Carstairs, sec. by A. Lorimer, 15 white, one black ....etc."

"In June 1887 a novel match was played between J.O.F. Morris, a son of Old Tom, and three members of the Club, Morris playing the best of the three balls. The match began at 11.30 p.m., in moonlight, and was followed by a large crowd of spectators. At no time was the light bright, and fore-caddies, equipped with umbrellas to protect them against being struck by balls, were employed to prevent balls being lost. Morris lost by two holes, but his score is interesting, and reads:-

Out, 555777635 - 50;

In, 434565656 - 44 - 94

A couple of policeman, seeing the crowd on the Links as the match was nearing home, thought something was wrong, and went out to make investigations.   The match ended at 3 a.m." (Robert Baptie).

Nov. 10th 1888

"Which night the clubs met in the Golf Hotel, Capt. W. Alexander in the chair, and entertained Mr. Petrie to a cake and wine banquet on account of presentation. Messrs. Stark & Ayton acted as Croupiers.   When after the usual Loyal and Patriotic toasts, the Captain W. Alexander presented Mr. Petrie with a very handsome marble timepiece in recognition of his services at the Ball.   In handing over the presentation the Capt. remarked that Mr. Petrie had been untiring in his efforts to make the Hall look at its best for the last few years.   Mr. Petrie in a very neat speech thanked the Club for the handsome present he had just got.   Then with toast, song and sentiment the Club spent one of its happiest evenings".

Dec. 14th 1888

"The Secy read a letter from J.L. Graham from America wanting some information on the game of golf and was instructed to send a Copy of the Rules of Golf and letter."

Dec. 17th 1889

The Secretary read a letter he had received from the Royal and Ancient Golf Club which was as follows:

"The Club House,

St. Andrews, N.B.

Gentlemen,

It will be within your recollection that at the autumn general meeting of this Club it was proposed and carried that the Royal and Ancient should present a medal to be played for annually by the members of the Artisan Clubs in the town. The Club accordingly instructed their jewellers to prepare designs, and these have now been received, and what appears to be a suitable one selected. The Club would, therefore, now invite you to formulate proposals as to the carrying out of the matter in detail. The points they would more particularly submit for your consideration are- 1st, What, if any of the Clubs besides the St. Andrews and Thistle should be eligible to compete; and, 2nd, at what time of the year should the competition take place? As to the latter point, I would suggest (but merely as a personal suggestion) that if it were to take place about the time the Royal and Ancient hold either their spring or autumn, a comparison of scores might prove interesting.

(Signed) H.S.C. Everard"

Jan. 3rd 1890

Our reply to this letter read:-

"The suggestions which the St. Andrews Golf Club would submit for your consideration are that the Medal be open to all Artisan Golf Clubs in the City. The St. Andrews and Thistle Golf Clubs only fulfilling these conditions.

The Foresters Club are debarred by their rules from any club competition.

The Fishermans Club are so exclusive that we know nothing of their rules - also -

That one member of the Thistle and one member of the St. Andrews Club play together and that it be played for the Saturday after your Spring Medal.

In submitting these our opinions through you to the Committee of the Royal & Ancient Golf Club whose practical knowledge and deep interest in the game are so well known we do so in the full assurance that their final arrangements will be such as to insure our hearty co-operation."

(The first winner was Alex Herd, later to win the Open in 1902.)

March 25th 1890

"It was also agreed that any Member leaving their work and carrying clubs in the Medal Week be suspended from the Club for Six Months. Or any member of the Club carrying clubs for three months be suspended from the Club for six months".

March 28th 1890

"Which night the General Meeting of the St. Andrews Golf Club was held in the Golf Hotel. Capt. Walter Alexander in the Chair, the Minutes of the previous meeting were read and agreed to. When A. Milne gave a few illustrations on the working of the Average system. After some discussion it was agreed to adopt the system. A. Milne moved, W. Stark seconded that the club play for charms in three classes, players lowering their average most to be the winners. W. Greig moved, G. Lorimer seconded, that the Club have a Tournament the same as a twelve months past summer and to be played in holes. On the Motion and amendment being put to the meeting

a Special Meeting of the Club
was Held in Mr Hastie's Inn
× Keys - 12th Janry 1853 -.
Captn in the Chair (Mr Howie
Better Known as Tow Head)
Present James Black -, a Galloway
Michard Lister. D. Clark.
a - Mc Phearson . W Ayton.
a Bruce. R. Paterson. J. Bruce.
a Clyne. John Hastie, J Keddie.
Elias Jones. Andrew Anderson.
J Martin. James Mc Phearson.
the Capt laid the following
document before the Meeting.

Moved by W Ayton, Seconded by
Jno Thomson , the Club agree
that Simply Strokes be Marked
on the Cards on Medal Days
the Secretary to Correct Strokes and
Sum up " agreed to, —.,

In 1890 William Ayton copied this extract from an 1853 Minute to confirm the correct method of marking cards with strokes not numerals. Not many club minutes refer to the Club Captain as "Towhead".

Walter Alexander

10 voted for amendment and 4 for Motion. Amendment carried, it was agreed that the entry money be 1/6 each".

May 9th 1890

"W. Greig moved, A. Milne, sec. on account of the Artillery having a turn out for drill and the members of Band be allowed to play from daylight to dark, ordinary hours to be from 2 till 4, members in the country ½ hour extra..... The Committee to meet at 7 o'clock and count cards, the general meeting to be at 8 o'clock when it was agreed to get 2 doz. of 3d. Pies, 2 doz. 2d. Tarts".

July 1st 1890

"Which night the St. Andrews Golf Club met in the Golf Hotel....when a letter was read from the Thistle Golf Club, St. Andrews, challenging us to a friendly match of 15 players aside which was agreed to accept if they would meet us in our Clubroom after the match for refreshments".

Robert Baptie tells of a break with tradition.

"The annual meeting of 19th September 1890 was a disastrous one from a sentimental point of view, as, after the officials had been elected and the arrangements made for the Medal, 'A discussion now arose as to the advisability of the Committee ordering pies and tarts for the meeting, ending in the result that this old custom be done away with.' For something like 45 years it had been customary for the Club to have a supper prior to presenting the prizes. Sometimes it was an elaborate affair, but most often the fare consisted of pies and tarts, which the Club always ordered. Whether it was a case of the members getting tired of pies or not, is not disclosed, but it certainly seems to have ended some of the sentimental interest in old customs."

"The stopping of the pies at the meeting when the prizes were presented only lasted a year, as at this meeting it was agreed to order two dozen 3d pies. While on the subject of pies, I was told a story related by an official of the Club who died a number of years ago. It was the custom of one of the members to keep his pie to take home with him, and usually there were pies left over, which were sold before the business was begun, and this particular member used to buy several more. During the course of the evening, someone would usually lift one or two from this member's stock when he was not watching, and when he discovered his loss, often when something was being discussed, the meeting was disturbed by a cry,

W. Greig

'Wha's ta'en my pies?' which was a signal for a burst of uproarious laughter from the rest of the members."

Sept. 29th 1890

"After distribution of prizes, the meeting was entirely given up to conviviality, numerous songs being sung and Healths proposed and drunk in flowing bumpers".

Nov. 1st 1890

"It was decided that canvassing for monthly donations and prizes be discontinued - prizes to be supplied from the Club funds and by members of the club who chose to do so.

The following members notified they would give prizes Capt. Ayton, J. Cleary - Canary bird, J. Angus, J. Pirie, D. Gourlay.

It was agreed that Allan Robertson's Club Box* which was offered to the Club on condition that it should be well taken care of be accepted and kept in the Golf Hotel.

There was lengthy discussion about the advisability of Medal Holders wearing their medals at the Ball, it was finally agreed that members please themselves."

* (This now stands just inside the Club's entrance.)

St. Andrews Golf Club 1892 with the Evening Times Trophy won by D. Simpson & W. Greig

Jan. 2nd 1893

"Mr Greig, Treasurer, intimated to the Club that he had received a handsome case of pipes from Mr. John Cleary to be played for."

The idea of providing a cup to celebrate the Club's fifty years was first raised in mid 1893 but the deliberations over the next months became increasingly complicated as you can see from the following sequence of extracts from the Minutes.

June 8th 1893

It was suggested the Club should try and raise a Jubilee Cup to be played for annually. The present Committee with the addition of A. Litster and W. Duncan were appointed to consider the matter.

Dec. 1893

For the Jubilee Cup. The Secy. reported the amount contributed to be £17.13.6. Mr. Wm. Ayton proposed, sec. by W. Alexander that a compulsory subscription of not less that 6d. per head be imposed on the Club members, so that the sum total might be raised to at least £20, which was agreed to by the Meeting; the Committee to carry out the necessary arrangements for the purchase of the Cup etc. and to submit same, to a G.M. of The Club for approval.

Feb. 10th 1894

For the Jubilee Cup - several sketches were submitted by Mr. Strath for the approval of the Committee by the different jewellers in St. Andrews; also from Mr. Greig of Kirkcaldy. The plan chosen was that submitted by Mr. Smith, South Street, subject to one or two alterations. It was decided that the height of the Cup be 14 ins. making a total of 20 ins. in height when placed on the stand. The Committee decided and instructed Mr. Strath to submit the plan with details to the various jewellers including Mr. Greig of Kirkcaldy.

March 21st 1894

"Mr. Strath informed the meeting that the design of the Jubilee Cup which had been chosen by the Committee and belonging to Mr. Smith, Jeweller, could not be obtained without payment of 15/-. It was, therefore, agreed by the Meeting that the design by Mr. Greig should be accepted on condition that he give the same weight of silver. It was thought some slight alterations on Mr. Greig's design would be advisable and it was left to the Committee to decide what should be done."

April 19th 1894

"A letter from Mr. Smith anent the Jubilee Cup design was read - pressing for payment of £1 for damage done to the design. The meeting agreed to reply courteously but stating that they must refuse to pay the sum requested."

June 18th 1894

"It was decided that a pine box stained walnut with handle and a good lock should be made to contain the Jubilee Cup, also a box for the reception of scoring cards to be placed in Tom Morris' shop - both to be made by Mr. Jas. Balfour.

The Secretary was instructed to notify on the Notice Board that the final of the Jubilee Cup must be played on or before Friday, 29th June."

June 28 1894

"The Committee also agreed to hand over the Jubilee Cup to the winner to retain in his possession for one year or so long as he holds it; and to have the Cup insured against theft and also that the runner-up in the competition for the Cup should be presented with a silver charm - a duplicate of the gold charm."

Aug. 20th 1894

"The Committee agreed not to insure the Jubilee Cup against theft; the insurance being too heavy, viz. 10/- per annum, but to continue the fire insurance." The first winner of the Jubilee Cup was Peter Anderson who had won the Amateur Championship the previous year. Did he realise as he accepted the trophy the long and earnest debate which had gone on in Committee about it?

Golf Inn, Aug. 21st 1894.

"The Committee met on the above night to consider how the Jubilee should be celebrated.... The Secy intimated that he had got the promise of a photo of Old Tom from Mr. Downie should a competition take place when W. Greig pro. and W. Duncan, sec. that a competition should be got up and a gold charm be the first prize and Old Tom's photo the second, with an entrance fee of 6d. and an optional sweep of 6d. which was agreed to. W. Ayton then proposed that a supper should take place and after a good deal of discussion owing to the Ball being so near this time and the Medal day and also it was thought the members would not turn out, finally a Committee consisting of A. Litster, W. Duncan, and Capt. Milne was appointed to carry out the arrangements provided they could get 30 members. A few names were then mentioned as to who the invited guests should be, namely Tom Morris, R. Forgan, George Bruce, Mr. Bennett and representatives from the University, Thistle, Leven and Carnoustie. W. Ayton pro. and Jas. Auchterlonie, sec. that the supper take place in the Cross Keys Hotel, no other business coming up, the meeting closed".

Golf Inn, Sept. 28th 1893.

"The Committee met on the above night. Capt. A. Milne presiding to allocate the odds and to ballot the members for the Autumn Medal and prizes which had been fixed for the 30th of September. A discussion arose as to whether the Club should send a notice of their Medal day to the Royal and Ancient as usual seeing that they had bought the land from Mr. Cheape. W. Greig proposed and A. Strath sec. that no notice be sent. Capt. A. Milne pro. and J. Liddel sec. an amendment that the Club take no notice of the purchase and send a notice as formerly. The amendment being carried the Secy was instructed to acquaint the R&A of the Club's Medal Day."

George Bruce joined the Club in 1847 and was Captain in 1855-6. He wrote books of poetry, history and bird life, was a talented actor, a prominent local politician and built the Bruce embankment at his own expense.

Golf Inn, Nov. 9th 1893.

"A general meeting of the St. Andrews Golf Club was held in the Golf Inn, Capt. A. Milne presiding..... The Ball Treasurer W. Marshall then gave in his report. The accounts showed an expenditure of £13.15.0d while the income only amounted to £9.12.0 showing a deficit of £4.3.0. Vice Capt. W. Ayton moved the adoption of the report but commented on the unsatisfactory state of the report, seconded by W. Greig. A good deal of discussion took place regarding the failure of the Ball as to how the accounts should be paid, the Club's Treasurer stating there was only 8/9d in the funds after taking out the £4.10.0. for the representatives expenses in the Times Trophy competition at Troon. Mr. A. Litster offered to make good the deficit by paying all the accounts giving the Club six months to repay him back without interest ..... Mr. Greig pro. that a levy 1/- per member should be put on the Club to meet the deficiency, sec. by A. Strath."

Golf Inn, Dec. 12th 1893.

"With regards to the Links purchase it was agreed on the motion of Mr. Ayton seconded by W. Greig that the document submitted before the Club and referring thereto be signed (assent) in favour of the 'Town Council'.

A letter from Sheriff Henderson was read before the meeting expressing a desire for a list of the membership of the Club and for a copy of its rules.

As the R & A had but recently intimated to the Club that all their correspondence ought to be conducted through their Secy. it was considered advisable to refuse the desired information unless applied for through the proposed source."

Dec. 21, 1893

"The Committee met in the Golf Inn to make the necessary arrangements for the competition on New Year's Day. It was decided that, instead of balloting members who intended to shoot, that they be placed by the Committee. - To strictly enforce that the members clear the books before being allowed to play. - That the entry money be 1/-, sixpenny sweep (optional). -

That in the event of there being water lying on the greens the ball be lifted and dropped behind the hazard without penalty; if bunkered in water, the penalty to be two strokes if the ball be lifted."

The loss on the Ball seems to have taken up the meeting's attention and as Robert Baptie reports:

"There is nothing in the minutes to indicate that the supper took place, but it is quite probable that it did. There was a great deal of talent in the Club, especially in the line of comic singers, and at all the suppers and presentations of prizes these members got full scope. One particular member who was always sure to get a place on the programme was John Gatherum, who, when he got started, could keep the company in fine humour. On one occasion, John was in a contrary mood, and absolutely refused to oblige the company, despite coaxing and threats. Not until one member got up and gave a contribution which did not please him, did he, immediately the member sat down, get up on his feet, announce that though he did not claim to be a singer, he thought he could better the last performance. There must have been some jealousy between the two, but my informant cannot remember who this particular member was. He told me that John's statement sent the company into fits of laughter, and that thereafter he excelled himself in the songs he sang."

"They had many happy evenings in those days, and it seems a pity that the atmosphere of these old gatherings cannot be re-captured now, for these gatherings did much to promote harmony among the members give them an opportunity to get together and know each other far better than by the present means of competitions."

It had been a momentous first fifty years for the Club. It had Allan Robertson and Tom Morris, who dominated the game in their day, as early members. The first Open Championship was at Prestwick in 1860. Old Tom Morris came second to Willie Park but then won it in 1861, 1862, 1864 and 1867.

Thereafter his son, "Young Tom", won in 1868, 1869 and 1870 and the original Belt became his property. After a gap of one year the present famous Claret Jug was put up in 1872 and Young Tommy won it again.

Apart from these eight wins, Andrew Strath won in 1865, Tom Kidd in 1873, Bob Martin in 1876 and 1885, Jamie Anderson in 1877, 1878 and 1879 and Willie Fernie 1883.

The Club had been greatly favoured in its office bearers. Our founding members quickly built up the Club with their initial enthusiasm, and anchor men like William Ayton, James Howie and George Bruce saw it thrive throughout the first splendid fifty years.

We were the right Club in the right place at the right time.

JUST A MINUTE (II)
(1894 - 1943)

The middle fifty years of our Club were eventful ones. In 1905 we purchased our first Clubhouse in Links Place. It was enlarged in 1922 when the property next door was acquired and in 1933 the decision to buy our present building was taken. The details are given in a separate chapter.

In this period our Committees had to face the problems created by two World Wars in addition to handling the considerable financial burdens which these purchases entailed.

Reading the Minutes you can smile occasionally at their niggardliness on some matters. They complained about the excessive use of electricity or the cost of our first telephone and watched the price of our coal bills. They did not suffer Bar Deficits gladly and Stewards who showed too many losses were shown the door without compunction. One Steward left owing the Club £30. When he died two years later the Club's lawyer was instructed to reclaim it from his estate if the opportunity arose.

These committees watched the pennies very carefully but when major decisions involving large capital expenditures on properties were required they took them quickly and decisively. They deserve our admiration and thanks.

By the 1890's St. Andrews Golf Club had become very powerful indeed. In the 1895 British Amateur Championship held in the town the winner, L. Balfour-Melville of the R & A, had to go to the 19th to beat W. Greig in the Quarter Finals and repeat this to defeat L. Auchterlonie in the Semi Final. It tells you something of the quality of their opponent that he defeated J. Ball, the best Amateur of the day and Open Champion that year in the Final.

The Evening Telegraph of 12/12/94 had this to say about us:

"A good deal has been written during the present year about the many brilliant golfers connected with the St. Andrews Club. On more than one occasion Mr. H. Hilton (who I should say, is about as competent a judge of golf as any one living) has favoured the readers of the Sporting Chronicle with "notes" regarding some of the more noted members of the Club, while several well-known writers on golfing matters have confirmed - what is pretty generally known throughout Fife and Forfarshire at any rate - the opinion that the members of the St. Andrews Club in the field of golf could give points to almost any other Society. It was stated in a Scotch newspaper not many weeks ago that twelve members of the St. Andrews Club could hold their own against twelve members of any other Club bar the Royal and Ancient. I think the latter Club might have been with safety included without doing very much damage to the reputation of the Artisan Club."

This picture of the second tee on the Old Course dates to around 1894

Hell Bunker one hundred years ago

65

Certainly we had a good conceit of ourselves as this letter from our Secretary illustrates:

To the Editor of The Golfer.

St. Andrews, 2nd April 1895

Sir,

I notice in your "English Notes" Column of last week an extract from the Sporting Chronicle, written by Mr. Hilton, anent the excellent scoring by the members of the St. Andrews Golf Club. Perhaps it may interest your readers to learn that, over a series of four competitions held on consecutive Saturdays, the scores of the first 12 men average 86 1-6th.

Taking into consideration the facts that on two of the Saturdays a troublesome wind blew, that the putting-greens, as is usual at this time of year, were very untrue, and that the competitions were the first after a long "lock-out" caused by the frost, the record is, without doubt, an exceptional one. With the green in its normal condition, the above average could by the same men be considerably reduced.

Whether these men could successfully cope with any other 12 players in the kingdom over a neutral green is, of course, difficult to say, but one thing is certain, and that is, to beat them their opponents would require to play golf.

I am, &c.,

Jas. Stewart, Hon. Secy.,

St. Andrews Golf Club.

The difference between self confidence and arrogance is a fine one. Our bold talk occasionally produced an acerbic response. H. Hilton, a prominent golfer and golf writer of the day, was not so enthusiastic about our claims.

Mr. Hilton, writing in the Sporting Chronicle, says, in regard to the St. Andrews Club, "A contemporary draws attention to the excellent scoring by the members of the St. Andrews Club in their competitions, and draws thereby somewhat odious comparison with the score sheets of our local clubs. He modifies the comparison, however, by remarking at the conclusion: "Of course we have to allow a little, as the circumstances of the players are slightly different." True, certainly, but hardly true enough, as the expression should have been: "We have to allow a great deal, as the circumstances are very different." Golf is, comparatively speaking, in its infancy in Manchester, and with the exception of a few Scotchmen, who have migrated south, the players in the district are all recruited from golfers who have taken up the game many years after the time in life which is the usually recognised limit for the making of a first-class player. The St Andrews Club (not to be confounded with the Royal and Ancient) is mainly recruited from the ranks of the artisan class and, as all the youth of St. Andrews take to golf as naturally as a duck to water, it is not to be wondered at that the average of play amongst the members is of a very high class. When in St Andrews, some two years ago, a member of the St Andrews Club made the statement to me that St Andrews could turn out twelve players (independent of the Royal and Ancient Club) who could hold their own with any other twelve players in the kingdom, if the match was played over St. Andrews. I have no doubt that the statement would be proved to be correct; but if played on a neutral green I hardly think they would prove so successful."

The 1897 match between ourselves and Forfarshire does confirm the depth of talent we had at that time as this contemporary newspaper report indicates.

GOLF

IMPORTANT MATCH AT MONIFIETH

St Andrews v. Forfarshire

What is probably the most important and interesting match that has yet been played on Monifieth Links came off on Saturday afternoon between teams representing the St Andrews Club on the one side and players selected from Clubs located in Forfarshire on the other. Mr. David Anderson of the Grange and Mr. William Young, the Secretary of the Monifieth Club, had most to do in getting up the contest and carrying through the arrangements. There was an evident desire on the part of the promoters to make the county team as representative of the various Clubs as possible, and places were allotted to members of the Monifieth, Panmure, Broughty, Dundee Advertiser, and Dundee Licensed Victuallers Clubs, while most of the Clubs who play on Carnoustie, Montrose, Arbroath, and Forfar had representatives forward. The course was specially prepared for the event, the tees being placed as far back as possible and on the most suitable sites, while the putting-greens were in good order. The strangers expressed satisfaction with the condition of the Links generally. The interested spectators either followed the players round the course or squatted on different parts of the Links, and made eager inquiries regarding the progress of the different couples as they passed.

FORFARSHIRE	Holes	ST ANDREWS	Holes
George Wright, Monifeith	0	I. Auchterlonie	0
David Bell, Carnoustie	1	J.C. Rose	0
Alex. Keillor, Montrose	4	William Greig	0
Robert Scott, Carnoustie	0	James Robb	4

Tom Morris on the first tee at the end of last century

St. Andrews Golf Club v Forfarshire 1897

Robert Winton, Montrose	0	James Anderson	7
Wm. Lorimer, Monifieth	0	Fred Herd	1
John G. Cobb, Montrose	4	W.A. Anderson	0
Wm. Hucheson, Monifieth	0	David Simpson	3
Alex. Cant, Carnoustie	2	Thomas Robb	0
W. Still, Dundee Advertiser	0	Robert Braid	0
Alex. Smith, Carnoustie	1	David Leitch	0
Jas. Findlay, Montrose	3	Walter Anderson	0
Jas. Simpson, Carnoustie	0	William Fogo	0
L.S. Smith, Montrose	1	Robert McAndrew	0
David Dargie, Monifieth	0	Thomas Auchterlonie	2
T. Jamieson, Carnoustie	0	Joe Auchterlonie	2
Charles Simpson, do.	0	A.F. Duncan	5
Robert Simpson, jun., do.	0	Peter Walker	2
J.C. Burns, Monifieth	0	James Kirk	3
Wm. Ballingall, Panmure	0	A.H. Manson	8
James Brodie, Forfar	0	Joe Mackie	8
J.B. Ballingall	0	Andrew Anderson	3
George Oswald, Broughty	0	George Braid	1
Wm. Young, Monifieth	7	Peter Craig	0
David Anderson, Panmure	0	Alexander Strath	3
Total	23	Total	52

Majority for St Andrews, 29 holes

ST ANDREWS INVINCIBLE

At the close of the match the players were entertained to a very substantial tea in the Literary Institute by Mr. David Anderson, who captained the county team. Mr. Anderson presided. After tea the Chairman expressed the pleasure he felt in seeing all the strangers present. The Monifieth Club had had many matches with their St. Andrews friends, but found they could never hold their own with them. It was thought that possibly with a combination such as they had that day they might come nearer the goal to which they aimed. The result, however, had shown them that the St. Andrews men were virtually invincible. There was hardly a Club in the world that could stand against them.   They all, he was sure, welcomed the St. Andrews men to Monifieth most heartily, and he hoped to meet them again on some future occasion. (Applause.)   In getting a team together he had been most ably assisted by Mr. Wm. Young, the Hon. Secretary of the Monifieth Club, who had performed the greater part of the clerical work.   The number of players in Forfarshire attached to 23 Clubs he computed at something like 4000, and out of these their team had been chosen.   The St. Andrews Club, on the other hand, nominally numbered 94 players, and the result of the match showed that the St. Andrews men were made of very good stuff.   They hoped, however, to bring together a better team to represent the county than they had had that day.

Ordinary Club members doubtless enjoyed the reflected glory of the team players but still took pleasure in the regular club competitions and the prizes which went with them.   The range and variety of prizes was considerable as this entry shows:

1st January 1895

17 prizes were distributed.

Mr. G. Bruce, 2 vols. value 20/-, Mr. Tom Stewart, Cleek and Iron value 11/-, Mr. McAndrew, Cleek head, A. Price, Bun 2/6. A. Wilson, Bun 2/6-, A. Dick, Picture, Mr. Berwick, Charm, Bob Martin, Club, Mr. Leslie, 1 Bott Whiskey & 1pt. wine, Mr. Suttie, Case Lemonade, J. Fleming, 1 Bott Whiskey, Bill Smart, Shortbread, K. Condie, 2 Iron heads, Mr. Niven, Duck & Hen, G. Lorimer, 1 Bott Whiskey.

The Starter's Box, Old Course

30th January 1895

"Capt. Stewart thereafter stated that it had been the wish of the Club that their honoured friend and fellow member, Mr. W. Ayton, should be the recipient of a small token of regard on his completion of 50 years connection with the Club. Vice Capt. Milne Thompson in a pithy speech presented Mr. Ayton with a handsome silver mounted walking stick bearing the following inscription. "Presented to Mr. W. Ayton by the members of St. Andrews Golf Club as a mark of their respect on his completing his 50th year as a member".

27th May 1895

"The first business before the meeting was the question of entering men in the Open Championship. After discussion it was moved by Mr. Rose and seconded by Mr. Milne that any member of the Club entering should do so at his own expense but should he finish in the first 12 and refuse to take a money prize his entry money be refunded by the Club".

6th August 1895

"A Long Driving Competition was held on this date and resulted as follows:

		yds.	ft.
1st	Wm. Anderson	222	1
2nd	L. Auchterlonie	220	2
3rd	D. Simpson	218	2

Conditions were best ball out of 3 to count. Roll included. Limit per width 60 yards".

20th August 1895

"It was agreed to hold an Approach Shot competition on Friday night the 30th at 6 o'clock. For Club members only. Entry money to go towards prizes. 3 balls to be played. Points to be given as follows. In hole 8, inside 1st ring 5, 2nd ring 3, 3rd ring 2".

3rd September 1895

"The question of approaching the Amateur Championship Committee regarding the rule making all clubmakers Professionals was discussed. It was the mind of the meeting that the rule was most unfair but the question was remitted to the Committee for their consideration and to take what action they thought best in the matter".

4th December 1895

"In the Secretary's report for 1895 were the following statements regarding the condition and doings of the Club.

Membership strictly revised	85
New members admitted	16

No. of Competitions		14
" " Rounds of the Links		23
Value of prizes	£ 21.10s	
" " sweeps	£ 16.14s	
Average net score of odds players		88.68
" " " " scr. "		86.89
Lowest score returned by L. Auchterlonie		75
Highest score		151
No. of Gen. meetings	6	
" " Com. "	13	
" " Odds Com. meetings	4	
" " Informal Com. meetings	33	

The Committee afterwards had an informal talk with Baillie Murray, a member of Green Committee anent the new rules to be issued by Green Committee. The Committee were unanimously of the opinion that 4 or 5 vacant places should be left in ballot places to be filled by those first on ground, that on Saturday afternoons ballot and vacant place should be alternate. These and others were discussed in a manner and spirit which Baillie Murray cordially approved and concurred with, agreeing with Committee's views so that he would have pleasure in laying same before Green Committee".

6th March 1897

"D. Leitch was not present to propose his Motion to abolish marking strokes on scoring cards during competitions. J. Robb, the sec. of Motion did not wish to press the Motion either but thought it would be better for the convenience of members and harmony of the Club itself to expressly state in Rule 5 that it is necessary to mark strokes as well as the totals taken to each hole. It was agreed to do so".

6th March 1897

"Jas Robb having won the clock presented to the Club by Alex. Herd, Huddersfield, was presented with the same by the Chairman who congratulated Mr. Robb in a few eulogistic remarks on his prowess as a golfer. Mr. Robb in acknowledging the prize expressed his satisfaction at winning. He was especially proud to win as the Prize was from one who was so famous in reputation as the donor. The Chairman intimated the probability of the Club being presented with a prize from another old member and celebrated golfer Willie Fernie, Troon, which would perhaps be competed for on March 20th".

13th March 1897

"A match took place today between teams got up by the Capt. and Secy. respectively;

the Capt's team winning by 2 holes, totals being 21:19. Old Tom, A. Kirkaldy and W. Auchterlonie being Honorary members took part in the match. A very enjoyable evening was afterwards spent in the Golf Hotel".

29th September 1898

"The Secy read a letter from Mr. Grace. Secy. of the Rules of Golf Committee, in answer to one he had written asking his Committee's ruling as to whether the St. Andrews Golf Club's committee were right or wrong in a decision they had given defining a stroke had to be marked when a player's ball had rolled from its position and rested in another as he was addressing his ball on the putting green although his club had not been grounded and he had not caused the ball to move.

The following is a correct copy of the reply received. "As the player did not touch the ball or, by touching anything, cause it to move, it was not a stroke and the decision of the Club Committee was wrong."

4th April 1899

"Attention was then called to a rule passed by the Royal and Ancient that the flag must be removed when within twenty yards of the hole and the following motion proposed by W. Greig, seconded by C. Grieve, was unanimously agreed to - viz. "That the rule recently passed by the Royal and Ancient that the flag must be removed when within twenty yards of the hole be not adopted in our own Club competitions."

6th February 1901

"It was agreed to refer to next Gen. Meeting Mr. Wedderburn's letter asking a contribution from the Club of 10/-, 15/- or 20/- yearly re agreement anent recovering balls from Station Master's garden". [This refers to what is now the Jigger Inn beside the Old Course Hotel]

27th February 1901

"Resolved - That in the event of James Nicoll, who has just returned from the War in South Africa, entering any Competition before next General Meeting, he be allowed to play".

18th April 1901

"The Secy read Mr. Wedderburn's letter asking a Subscription from the Club of 10/-, 15/-, 20/- anent getting access to Station Garden. Wm. Greig moved, sec. by A. Cummings, "That 5/- be given." J. Angus moved, sec. by R. Wallace, not to subscribe for the object contemplated. On a division Motion and Amendment each received 5 votes, when the Chairman gave his casting vote in favour of J. Angus's motion".

18th May 1902

"Mr. R. Wallace proposed that "As the 24th May was the date of the Inspection of the Volunteer Artillery, Artillerymen be allowed the privilege of playing on the Thursday previous to the 24th, and that they be allowed only to play on that day and not on the

Saturday, and that no member except he be an artillery man be allowed to play on the Thursday. This the meeting agreed to".

10th October 1902

"It was proposed by A. Dewar, sec. by R. Scott that we do not give the Starter the usual honorarium of 2/6d as he did not give the members any fair play in Starting on Saturday competitions. Amendment by R. Wallace, sec. by J. Sutter that the Starter get his usual honorarium. The motion was carried by a majority. It was agreed to give the greenkeepers the usual honorarium of 4/-".

25th December 1902

"It was resolved to hold the usual competition on New Years Day 1903. There was some discussion as to the place of meeting, to distribute the prizes won on New Years Day owing to the order of Magistrates to close all Licensed Houses on that day. It was proposed if possible to hold one meeting on New Year's Day so as not to let old custom of meeting be broken".

13th May 1903

"Proposed by R. Robertson, sec. by R. Wallace, that we do not give our usual order for clubs to Messrs. Forgan but give the order to our own members, Messrs. Auchterlonie & Anderson and Sons. Carried".

7th October 1903

"Proposed by R. Wallace that medal prizes be divided between T. Morris & D. & W. Auchterlonie & Anderson & Sons, Sec. G. Stewart. As an amendment by T. Melville that Forgan & Son get their share. Sec. by Jas. Davidson. Motion carried".

11th May 1904

"Mr. I. Walker having, on account of ill health, been unable to work and being playing and carrying for a few, Mr. A. Litster moved that Mr. Walker be allowed to play for the Medals; and that this case be made a precedent for guidance as in classing men unable to work with men out of work as mentioned in Rule of Management No. 13".

25th June 1904

"This day the Monthly Competition for the Diamond Jubilee Medal was played in almost perfect weather. Mr. Simpson was first, his score of 74 establishing a record for score play on St. Andrews Links. Details of score Out: 3 5 5 4 5 4 4 3 4 = 37

In: 4 2 4 4 6 4 5 5 3 = 37 "

8th December 1904

"In regard to the Club's matches for the incoming year, it was resolved, on the motion of Mr. D. Simpson, seconded by T. Young, to play the usual matches. It was moved by Mr. D. Simpson and seconded by Mr. A. Dewar, to revert to the old system of counting by holes in the matches. There being no amendment the motion was declared carried.

The Secretary was empowered to arrange suitable dates, and on the suggestion of R. Scott was asked to state that this Club only play against a purely Amateur Team".

12th April 1905

"The handicapping Committee met on this date in the Golf Hotel when the question of plussing the scratch players was raised. Mr. A. Dewar proposed and Mr. R. Scott seconded that the scratch players to be plussed and this was unanimously agreed to. The odds book was then gone over and it was agreed to plus Messrs. James Anderson, William Greig, A. Gallacher, David Anderson & David Simpson by 2 shots".

There is a Minute dated 7th August 1905 which starts "The Committee met this evening in the Club House, Mr. R. Wallace in the Chair." It must have been a most satisfying moment for our Secretary to be able to write "in the Clubhouse."

Immediately thereafter there is a noticeable change in our Club Minutes. Before 1905, they concern themselves largely with golf and social matters. After 1905 the problems of running the new building occupy a large part of our records. The week to week organising of competitions was left to a Golf Committee which occasionally led to friction between it and the main committee.

4th February 1908

"Tournaments. The following were appointed to arrange Domino and Push Halfpenny Tournaments, viz. Messrs. Millar (Convener), Law, Grieve and Scott".

5th May 1908

"Card Playing. The Secretary was instructed to put up a notice in the Club to the effect that complaints having been made to the Committee regarding the noise made by some junior members of the Club and that in future apprentices and junior members are requested not to play cards in the main Club Room but may do so in a room upstairs provided for that purpose and that no playing of cards for money or cigarettes will be permitted on the Club premises by junior members".

7th August 1909

"Tea sets, etc. left over from Bazaar. Mr. Singer offered 10/-for these but it was decided to hold on for a bit".

14th September 1909

"Professionals. Mr. D. Auchterlonie moved that any member who becomes Professional for time being shall be debarred from playing in Club's competitions. On returning to work for one month, however, he shall again be allowed all the privileges of the Club".

7th October 1909

"At St. Andrews the seventh day of October nineteen hundred & nine.

At an Extraordinary General meeting of St. Andrews Golf Club, Mr. Bell in the Chair. After considerable discussion as to whether Professionals be allowed to compete in all competitions, a ballot was taken, when it was carried by a large majority that Professionals be allowed to play in all competitions".

21st October 1909

"The Chairman reported that Mr. Munro had sent to the Club a new <u>curling rink apparatus</u> which he was willing to sell the Club for £2. After considerable discussion it was agreed to instruct the Secretary to thank Mr. Munro for his offer but to decline same as they thought it would inconvenience members reading". [This may have been a miniature curling rink for use indoors. The "stones" ran on ball bearings.]

"Fires - It was agreed to instruct the Steward to start the fires on Saturday first, 23rd October".

9th November 1909

"It was agreed to instruct Steward to sell his existing stock of 3d and 4d cigars at 2d as they were getting dry".

14th December 1909

"Leak in beer pipe. A letter was read from Steward stating that a burst had occurred in which he had lost six gallons of beer. The pipe being lead was not convenient and it was agreed to have a rubber pipe substituted. The Sec. was asked to instruct Mr. Auchterlonie to have this supplied. It was also agreed to allow the Steward for loss of above six gallons beer". [I wonder if our beer drinkers noticed a subtle change of flavour.]

"At St. Andrews the first day of February 1910. In a meeting of St. Andrews Golf Club Extraordinary General Meeting, Mr. J.S Bett, Chairman. The Chairman explained to meeting that on account of a request by the Town Council that a continuous ballot be tried over the Old Course for say three months in the summer, the R & A (Green Committee) had requested other clubs interested to send a representative to a meeting on 25th January to consider the matter.

The Chairman explained that he had attended that meeting and explained that Mr. Rutherford had proposed that ballot be from 9-11.30 and from 1-5. The R & A were willing to try the ballot in July and if a success perhaps August but on no account would they agree to ballot in September.

Mr. Singer moved that the St. Andrews Golf Club be in favour of continuous ballot for times stated but would ask if it was not possible to ballot from 12.30 on Saturdays, seconded by James Young. It was unanimously agreed that it would be better if no starter were employed after 5 o'clock. Mr. Hill was asked to represent the club at meeting to be held on 2nd February to reconsider the whole question".

12th April 1910

"Mr. Singer moved that the Professionals should be allowed free use of Billiard table during the Championship week - seconded by Mr. G.L. Munro".

15th April 1910

"Mr. H.M. Singer moved that this year the team playing against Carnoustie get their train fares paid - seconded by Mr. G.L. Munro. Mr. D. Auchterlonie expressed the view that it was a poor spirit to encourage in the Club, he however did not wish to put an amendment".

H. Singer

10th May 1910

"Mr. Singer proposed that some little encouragement be given to those professionals who might find themselves out of the running early in the week and he signified his willingness to put up a silver cup and take his chance of the 1/- entry. After considerable discussion it was agreed to do nothing in the matter. The Secretary reported that he had written the Secretary of Golf Agency to the effect that the club would be at disposal of professionals during Championship week and that as there was a good billiard table it might add to the week's enjoyment. A reply was read acknowledging same and stating that they intend giving a prize of £1.10 and two of 5/- for a billiard handicap amongst the professionals".

28th October 1911

"Mr. Guy C. Campbell intimated, per D. Auchterlonie, that he intends gifting the Club with a Medal and Cup. The former he suggested should be called the Coronation Aggregate Medal and Cup be played for in foursomes as near the 18th January as possible to commemorate the birth of twins".

13th January 1911

"The Secretary was instructed to write Mr. Guy Campbell a letter and thank him for the handsome silver challenge bowl and silver charms which had arrived and to ask him if he would consent to becoming an Hon. Member of the Club".

14th April 1911

"Mr. Greive moved that in future all Foreign members be liable for their full subscription provided they intended playing in Club competitions, otherwise they be entered as temporary members for the six months at 5/-. Seconded by Mr. H.M. Singer".

8th September 1911

"Mr. Greive moved that the bath charge be reduced to 3d. Seconded by R. Scott".

10th November 1911

"A letter was read from J.R. Stewart on behalf of Ball Committee requesting that the cups, medals, pictures, etc. belonging the club be taken to Town Hall on 17th curt. for decoration purposes and also asking them to close the Club an hour earlier on that night. Mr. Singer moved that the request as regards the cup and pictures be granted on condition that the Ball Committee be responsible for their safety while out of Club, seconded by T. Melville.   Mr. J. Liddel moved that the Club be shut at usual time, seconded by J. Petrie.   J. Elder moved that the Club be shut an hour earlier as requested.   Seconded by H.M. Singer.   On a show of hands the motion was carried".

13th August 1912

"A considerable amount of discussion took place regarding the non-serving of liquor at bar while meetings were being conducted.   It was finally agreed to keep bar open, but members to be requested not to hang about the bar and also that the door between large room and cycle house be closed while meeting is in progress.   On motion of Mr. Watson, seconded by J. Liddel, the Secy. was instructed to submit a monthly statement of the drawings at bar, money in Steward's hands, etc. and balance in bank.

The question of having a telephone in Club was discussed but it was not thought advisable to do anything in the matter".

13th December 1912

"On suggestion of the Secy. it was agreed to hinge the lavatory door on right side of opening and have a bench fixed at back of door for members cleaning their clubs".

10th January 1913

"On motion of Mr. Dixon, seconded by J. Elder, it was agreed that the fire in Billiards room be set so that members might light same if they thought fit during indifferent weather.   The Secretary reported that he had arranged this".

6th February 1913

"Mr. Dixon pointed out that the Caretaker's conduct for some time past had not been what it should have been and that the Club was not kept as clean as it might be.   Mr. Liddel pointed out that the windows gave one the idea that the place was uninhabited. The Secretary was instructed to advertise for a Caretaker, married (with no encumbrances preferred) in Citizen, Scotsman, Dundee Advertiser and Courier.   Salary £40 per annum with free house, coal & gas.   Applications to be addressed to Secy. and delivered along with three testimonies by Saturday 22nd curt".

12th May 1913

"The Fire Insurance policy was looked into when it was agreed to have the undermentioned cups etc. included, viz".

Jubilee Cup	£25
Hugon Cup	£12
Guy C. Campbell	£5
Haig Cup	£10
McGregor Trophy	£5
	£57

31st July 1913

"The Chairman made a few remarks and complimented the members on the continuous prosperity of the Club, but he considered the tariff on Golf Courses might tell on our membership in the future, and he thought a combined effort by the local clubs should be made to secure a greater consideration from the Town Council".

14th October 1913

"The Captain reported that he and the Secretary had had an interview with the Finance Committee of Town Council, when he explained how the proposed Tariff was to affect this Club. The Provost promised to give the matter due consideration and possibly another interview would be necessary to go into details. Mr. W. Watson who had been at the meeting complimented Mr. Dixon on the able speech he had made on behalf of the Club".

9th December 1913

"The Secretary was instructed to inform Steward to see that spittoons were cleaned out regularly".

13th January 1914

"The Secretary read a letter he had received from Town Clerk intimating that Town Council had agreed to allow 20 non-resident bone fide members to play over golf courses on payment of £1 each. A certificate to this effect to be granted by the Secretary. The tickets to be granted to the above 20 members will be available on the Old and New Course. It was agreed that the members so affected should be notified and requesting that they let us know if they intend taking advantage of the rebate - otherwise the places might be filled up by others".

27th January 1914

"The Secretary read a letter he had received from Peter Walker, Alloa, re tariff. It was agreed that the Secretary should reply in as curt terms as possible

The question of boys coming into Club to clean members' clubs was discussed when it was agreed that Steward be instructed to keep an eye on same".

10th March 1914

"The Captain reported that Mr. Cargill Cantley had asked him to go to Cupar to give evidence in favour of Town Council in connection with the Bye Laws for Links but pointing out that he had refused as he could not adequately express the sentiments of the members of the St. Andrews Golf Club".

There is no direct reference in the Minutes to the outbreak of the First World War or indeed to the end. It is remarkable how little mention is made throughout the four years of the most devastating conflict the world had seen.

Other records show that around 70 of our members served in the Armed Forces and seven lost their lives. They won a variety of medals including a Croix de Guerre but only one is recorded formally - the VC won by Sergeant John Ripley.

Competitions and inter club matches were abandoned but the Club continued functioning though shortages of beer and whisky supplies caused members problems.

11th September l914

"A letter from Messrs. Thomson & Cantley on behalf of the Prince of Wales A.R. Fund was submitted when it was agreed to head a subscription list with £3.3/- and hang same up in large room so that members might have an opportunity of subscribing thereto.

It was also agreed to give £1.1/- to the Belgian Fund. It was suggested to take half of sweep money in the Autumn Comp. to hand over to the Prince of Wales Fund but after due consideration it was agreed to let the matter drop".

12th April 1915

"The following resolution was adopted, proposed by Mr. R. Scott and seconded by Mr. Thos. Liddel. That members of the Club serving in the Army or the Navy during this war, should not be called upon to pay their Annual Subscription until the May following their return, and the Secretary was requested to send a copy of this resolution to all such members".

29th July 1915

"It was intimated that over 40 members of the Club were at present serving in the Army and Navy and it was decided to have a Roll of Honour made and exhibited in the Club. It was left in the hands of the Committee to arrange for a permanent tablet being placed in the Club at the end of the war giving the names of Members who had served". [There is no further mention of this in the Minutes.]

5th August 1915

"It was agreed to insure the Property and Furnishing of the Club against Bombardment and Aircraft to the same amount as the Fire Insurance Policy and the Captain and Secretary were authorised to see Messrs. Thomson & Cantley and arrange this provided the Premium was not to exceed 3/6d per £100.

It was agreed to admit soldiers as Temporary Members at 2/- per month if proposed and seconded by two Members of the Club, the latter to be responsible for the conduct of such Temporary Members in the Club".

12th October 1915

"A sum of Ten shillings and six pence was voted from the Club funds towards Sergt. Ripley V.C. Testimonial and Messrs. Thos. Liddel and D. Jolly undertook to collect further subscriptions from the Club members".

9th May 1916

"Owing to the high price of matches it was decided that matches for the use of Club members should only be placed in the stand in front of the Bar".

13th December 1917

The Secretary intimated a prize of 30 Tons of Coal from Lieut. Colonel J.T. Champion, Hon. Vice-President of the Club, for competition among the members. It was decided to hold the Competition on New Year's Day and to make 8 Prizes as follows:- 8, 6, 5, 4, 3,, 2, 1, 1 bags of Coal, also that the 6d. sweep be divided into 6 prizes of equal value.

17th April 1918

"A circular letter was read from Messrs. George Younger & Son stating that the beer would be curtailed to one third of the supply in 1915 and asking the Club to make arrangements for economy in the consumption of the beer. The Secretary was instructed to inform the Caretaker regarding this matter".

25th July 1918

"It was decided to discontinue the Aircraft and Bombardment Insurance on the Club premises".

9th January 1919

"After considerable discussion regarding the rationing of the sale of whisky and other spirits in the Club, it was decided that during the present shortage no member should be allowed more than one glass per day, with the exception of Saturday when two glasses should be the limit, and the Secretary was instructed to place a notice in the Bar to this effect".

The Club holds a series of Press cuttings covering the year 1919. These provide an entertaining and informative picture of the St. Andrews Golf Club getting back into action after the War years.

The annual battle with Carnoustie was resumed with all its old enthusiasm. As a preamble to the 1919 match the reporter recalled the series of games leading up to the War and particularly the 1914 contest.

"It is interesting to note that several of the St. Andrews players who took part in that great match will be playing at Carnoustie on Saturday. They are L. Auchterlonie, W. Greig, Jas. Anderson, David Simpson, T. Melville, and Geo. Braid.

In addition to those already mentioned, famous players such as Alex Herd, Fred McKenzie, and A. Gallagher have at different times taken part in the Carnoustie match, and on the Carnoustie side R. Harris, Dr. F.H. Scroggie, David Robertson, P. Robertson, D.G. Soutar, Stewart Maiden, and Fred Brand are names which have won fame in the amateur and professional world.

For the first twenty years of the match St. Andrews proved invincible, but from 1901 to 1913 Carnoustie got a bit of their own back and during that period claimed success after success, and became rightly regarded as the greatest side in the land. In

1913 St. Andrews again came into its own, Carnoustie being conquered that year and again in 1914, so that Saturday's encounter - coming after a lapse of five years - is of special interest and has a delightful element of uncertainty about it.

The St. Andrews side has a splendid quartette to lead off with. In. L.B. Ayton, L. Auchterlonie, Jas. Anderson, and Geo. Ayton are four players of great reputation and experience.

Since his return to his native town L.B. Ayton has shown marvellous form. His scores round the Old Course border on the superlative, as witness his 69 the other evening and two 72's in one day. Ayton had a great reputation before he left St. Andrews to turn professional. That reputation he enhanced during his sojourn in the South, first with the Bishop Stortford Club and latterly with the Rye Club. He represented Scotland in the Professional Internationals of 1910, 1912, and 1913, and won the "Evening Telegraph Cup in 1906. Incidentally he has beaten J.H. Taylor every time he has met him. Now be bids fair to still further add to his reputation, and in him we have a probable open champion. Only 34 years of age, he is a modest, well set-up fellow, liked by all. He will be the great attraction in Saturday's battle.

L. Auchterlonie is second only to Ayton at St. Andrews, and although in the veteran stage - he is now 51 - his form week in week out is splendid. In competition scores of 75 and 76 are quite common occurrences with him, and but for Ayton's superlative form he would be once again leading the St. Andrews side today. An ex-open champion of America, he won the "Evening Telegraph" Cup away back in 1897 and today is playing as well as ever. A keen player and a warm supporter of the Carnoustie-St. Andrews match.

Jas. Anderson has won every golfing honour St. Andrews has to bestow. A fine player, with a graceful action, Anderson is always delightful to watch. Like L. Auchterlonie, a veteran in this historic match, and very keen. As yet no sign of "Anno Domini" about his golf. Aged 49, and a real son of St. Andrews.

Geo. Ayton, brother of L.B. A coming player who has been doing well all season. Is not new to the match, and has worthily earned his high place in the team.

Willie Greig, hero of a hundred fights. The man who never tore up a card in his life. Perhaps the hardest man to beat in match play, as Mr. Hilton can testify. Has played against Carnoustie for 30 years, and is still a great player. Has the match very clearly at heart, and is a real type of the hard-working artisan amateur golfer.

David Simpson, the "doyen" of the team. A grand player in his day and still worthy of inclusion in the side. Has played against Carnoustie for close on 40 years now, and is still as keen as ever. Brother of Bob Simpson, Carnoustie.

In Geo. Braid, T. Melville, and A Cumming we have players long experienced in these matches, who will help to balance the side. The St. Andrews side contains a good many young and promising players, new to the match, who are confidently expected to give a good account of themselves. Granted a fine day the match is sure to be a great attraction."

It must have been something of a shock when our team went down by 13 matches to 7 at Carnoustie. However, it set the scene for the return match at St. Andrews.

"Tomorrow (Saturday) the St. Andrews Club have a visit from the powerful Carnoustie team in the return inter-Club fixture. The match will be played over the Old Course, for which priority of start has kindly been granted from 1 p.m. to 3 p.m.

Carnoustie travel with the useful lead of 6 points - 13 to 7 being the verdict at Carnoustie on 17th May last; but the local side hope to wipe out that margin tomorrow on their own 'Midden heid.' It will take a bit of doing, however, for the Carnoustie side is strong from top to bottom.

St. Andrews have chosen a very strong 25, including 11 plus men, and if they fail to win tomorrow then there must surely be something wrong with their golfing temperament. Both sides show changes from that which did duty at Carnoustie - changes which strengthen the sides, so a battle-royal should be witnessed.

St. Andrews are including the three brothers Kyle, a welcome appearance being E.P. Kyle, the hero of the 1913 Amateur Championship, Tait medal winner 1913-1914, and who reached the 6th round of the Dundee Evening Telegraph Cup at St. Andrews in 1912. E.P. is at present in the Army, but he will be ready for the fray tomorrow. Denys Kyle, the 'Varsity champion, is following fast on the heels of his more famous brother, and R.B. is shaping likewise. The trio add considerable strength to the side tomorrow.

L.B. Ayton will lead the team, and his reputation is already too well known to need repetition here. He meets Jas. Mason the Carnoustie crack, but I fancy Ayton.

L. Auchterlonie, especially after his brilliant performance last Saturday, will have a following in his match with F.S. Gallett, who has made a jump from playing 11th at Carnoustie to 2nd at St. Andrews.

With Jas. Anderson, Geo. Ayton, G. Braid, W. Fowlis, A.C. Taylor following the two leaders in the order named, St. Andrews have truly a galaxy of talent at the top, and as they did not fail at Carnoustie we hardly expect them to do so at home tomorrow.

In the Carnoustie side the newcomers are:- W. Dorward, the St. Mirren F.C. player (who won the Footballers' Championship at Troon last week), W. Fotheringham, J.Y. Watson, J.L.B. Robertson, and J.S. Dargie, and all make for strength. Great interest is being taken in the match, not only in Tayside and St. Andrews circles, but outside, and excitement is running high.

A fine day is what everyone is praying for to ensure the grand historic fixture being the success it deserves. The following are the respective sides:-

	ST. ANDREWS		CARNOUSTIE	
1.	L.B. Ayton	(plus 6)	Jas. Mason	(plus 3)
2.	L. Auchterlonie	(plus 5)	F.S. Garrett	(plus 1)
3.	Jas. Anderson	(plus 4)	J.R. Hosie	(sc.)
4.	Geo. Ayton	(plus 4)	W.R. McKay	(sc.)
5.	G. Braid	(plus 4)	T. Walker	(sc.)
6.	D.H.Kyle	(plus 2)	J.C. Stuart	(sc.)
7.	W. Fowlis	(plus 2)	A.C. Ogg	(sc.)
8.	E.P. Kyle	(plus 2)	J.B. Cunningham	(sc.)
9.	A.C. Taylor	(plus 1)	J.A. Garrett	(sc.)
10.	J. Anderson	(sc.)	J. Campbell	(sc.)
11.	W. Greig	(sc.)	W.S. Whyte	(sc.)
12.	J. Melville	(sc.)	W. Dorward, jun.	(sc.)
13.	J. McIntosh	(plus 2)	A. Scott	(sc.)
14.	G. Gourlay	(sc.)	K. Black	(sc.)
15.	T.F. Currie	(sc.)	W. Fotheringham	(sc.)
16.	J. Sorley	(sc.)	J.S. Dargie	(sc.)
17.	L. Gourlay	(plus 2)	J.Y. Watson	(sc.)
18.	J.R. Brown	(sc.)	A.D. Crerer	(1)
19.	R.B. Kyle	(sc.)	W.B. Crerer	(1)
20.	T. Melville	(sc.)	J.L.B. Robertson	(1)
21.	John Auchterlonie	(sc.)	W. Grieve	(2)
22.	J. Mackie	(sc.)	Jas. Murray	(2)
23.	J. Suttie	(sc.)	W.B. Richardson	(1)
24.	M. Stewart	(4)	G. Bothwell	(1)
25.	D. Simpson	(4)	E. Gibson	(2)"

Fortunately the St. Andrews team which looked so formidable on paper did, in fact, prove to be equally formidable on the golf course.

19th July 1919
"GOLF GOSSIP"
By our St. Andrews Correspondent

St. Andrews Club's Great Triumph over Carnoustie

Locals Win by 18 - 7 at Home

The great inter-Club battle between St. Andrews and Carnoustie, the two most powerful match-playing Clubs in the whole country, has resulted in a wonderful triumph for the St. Andrews Club.

Last Saturday over the Old Course, and in presence of a spectatorate numbering quite 2000, the St. Andrews Club wiped out the 6 points deficit recorded in the first half of the match at Carnoustie, and converted it into a splendid triumph of 5 matches on the home-and-home.

The St. Andrews Club had selected a powerful team to duty last Saturday; indeed, it is a moot point whether in all its long and wonderful career the Club ever had such a strong side out. Of the 25 matches no fewer than 18 wins were registered, and had the result been decided by the old system of holes up, St. Andrews would have had a sweeping success. As it is, 18-7 is a quite sufficient margin, and there were no halved matches. The weather was favourable on the whole, despite occasional heavy showers which came on between one and two p.m. but they needed to take the fire out of the greens. As showing the interest taken in the match, Press photographers 'snapped' the leading players as they departed from the first teeing ground.

So St. Andrews not only won by a splendid margin but converted a 6 points defeat into a 5 points win on the home and home, and this is their fourth successive success over their great rivals. The team thoroughly justified the confidence bestowed on it, and as at present constituted is there another side in the whole country to match it? I really think that a special group of the team should be taken, to hang side by side with the team which accounted for the chosen of Forfarshire away back in 1898, for the present lot have worthily maintained the reputation of the Club, made and handed down by the Forfarshire victors so long ago. Of such stuff are our future Scottish champions made.

The following month saw one of that successful team bring back a major trophy to the St. Andrews Club.

2 August 1919

"The handsome Dundee Evening Telegraph Cup has been so many years out of St. Andrews that one had begun to despair of it being brought back to the city again. Not since 1906, when L.B. Ayton secured it at Burntisland, has this much-prized trophy found a resting place in the Ancient City. Happily, St. Andrews can still raise first-class golfers, and Denys Kyle is the latest player to land the cup in St. Andrews and add further lustre to the golfing reputation of the city. He is a worthy winner in every respect and great was the rejoicing in St. Andrews on Saturday night when the tidings spread that he had won. Had the cup gone to Carnoustie that place would have been decorated; the local band would have turned out to play the winner to the Clubhouse, and the Peace celebrations simply wouldn't have had a look in. As it was, Kyle got a quiet but none the less warm reception when he arrived back from Montrose last Saturday night bringing the cherished cup with him.

Friend Singer was a 'prood, prood' man, as he made his way down to the St. Andrews Club, holding high the cup, while the winner dodged his waiting friends, and crept out of the station by the back way. In the St. Andrews Club a host of the members assembled to greet the winner, and in no time the cup was filled amid great cheering, and the health of the winner (and other people's health) cordially pledged."

The same year also had some lighter moments reported.

28 May 1919

"SPRING CLEANING AT ST ANDREWS

Fire Engine at Work on the Old Course

The worms have lately proved rather plentiful on the greens of the Old Course, St. Andrews, the 18th green being perhaps the worst, so it was decided to try and mitigate the nuisance.

Some genius hit on the idea of employing the town steam fire engine to pump salt water from the sea to the last green.

The experiment duly came off late on Friday evening last.

Soon the green was liberally soaked with the salt water - so were some of the spectators - while Tom Morris' shop opposite got a thorough washing.

In a very short time up wriggled worms of all sizes and the green was soon a mass of perforations and crawling worms. Andrew Kirkaldy was delighted. 'Talk about worm-killer!' he shouted, "that bates a'your worm-killers.'

After about an hour and a half of pumping operations the engine was shut off, and Kirkaldy got a willing band of juveniles to clean the dead worms off the green.

Thousands of dead worms were removed, and altogether the work proved a great success.

It could be repeated with benefit at some of the other greens.

The Old Course is now closed for a fortnight's rest and overhaul in view of the coming big professional event next month, and I am confident it will be in fine playing condition when the great masters of the game come north."

The August Medal on the Eden Course obviously did not qualify as a lighter moment -

9th August 1919

LOCAL GOLF GOSSIP
St Andrews Club Members v. Eden Golf Course

By way of a change, the St. Andrews Club members chose the Eden Course last Saturday for their August monthly medal competition. The day was an exceedingly unpropitious one, for a very boisterous westerly wind prevails, which made this exacting course very very difficult and many tales of lost balls and lost tempers were unfolded.

Nevertheless 78 cards were taken out, but only 31 were returned for scrutiny, and many players failed to stay the full course. Scoring was high, yet there were three very fine cards handed in by L.B. Ayton, John Melville and Frank Hoy. Each went round in 80, which represented great golf under the conditions.

J.S. Mentiply proved to be the winner with 84, less 7-77. Result - More 'docking' of his liberal handicap allowance.

'Nae mair of ye'r .... Eden Course for me!' gloomily remarked a player who had lost five balls out where the whins and heather abound, and the wind rushes down the Eden estuary. The Eden Course tests a player's accuracy in every department of the game, but I still think the short 14th a most unfair hole."

23rd April 1920

"A letter was read from the Secretary R & A Golf Club offering a picture of the late Tom Morris when it was agreed to accept same and thank the R & A for same".

8th February 1921

"An enjoyable Smoking Concert was held in the Club Room on Tuesday 1st inst. in honour of our American Members at present on a visit to St. Andrews. The finances of this entertainment were raised by subscription but unfortunately the expenses exceeded the income by £1.15.4. The Captain generously made good the deficiency. On the Motion of Mr. Rutherford, the Captain and Mr. D. Blair were thanked for the active part they took with the arrangements. It was decided to suggest for the benefit of future Committees that any such entertainment be by ticket".

In February 1922 the death of James Sorley, Match Secretary, was noted. Thanks to his enthusiasm for the history of the Club we have details about its early years which would otherwise have been lost. Robert Baptie, another enthusiast, speaks well of him. "I think Mr. Sorley was one of the best members the Club has had and by his flights into journalism he brought St. Andrews Golf Club prominently before

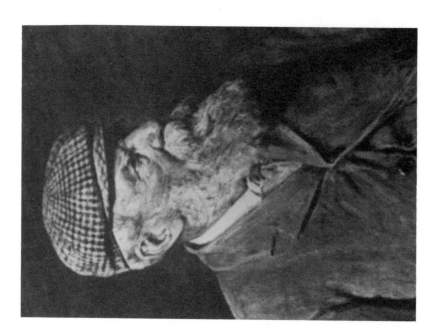

Tom Morris

A. Robertson's Locker

the golfing community. 'Jimmy' was a loveable fellow and it is very fitting that his portrait hangs in the Clubhouse among the portraits of those who have rendered outstanding service to the Club in the past". This was written in 1933.

13th March 1923

"A letter from Mr. J. McAndrews, Secretary of the Scottish Section of the Professional Golfers' Association was submitted. The Qualifying stage for the Scottish Section of the Daily Mail Competition is to be held at St. Andrews on 12th April, and it was suggested by the professionals that a match of 30 players a side might be arranged between them and St. Andrews Club on the previous evening. The Secretary was instructed to write offering the privilege of the Club to all the professionals for the event, and stating that the Committee would endeavour to get a team to meet them".

1st May 1923

"The Meeting was called in connection with a disturbance that occurred in the Clubhouse on Saturday 28th April. It appeared that a street violinist had come into the Club and had been encouraged by some members to play. On the other hand, the majority of the members present objected to the intrusion. The Secretary informed the player that he must leave the Club. Mr. J.Y. a member, refused to accept this ruling and the Secretary appealed to Mr. Spence, Capt. of the Club, who was in the Billiard Room. The Captain at once went to the Bar Lounge and requested the violinist to leave the premises. While waiting for the "Visitor" to leave the Captain was accosted by Mr. Y who also challenged his authority and gave him a blow in the face. At the same instant Mr. T.S. who had just come into the Club also hit Mr. Spence and a disturbance ensued. A letter was read to the meeting from Mr. Spence regarding the above. After consideration the Committee unanimously decided to suspend Mr. Y and Mr. T.S. from the Club pending an extraordinary General Meeting and the Secretary was instructed to notify these members of the decision".

5th June 1923

"The Boys' Championship organised by St. Andrews Golf Club was a very successful event. The keen interest taken in the competition by the general public also proved its popularity. An entry of 49 was received, the ages varying from over 14 to under 18 years.

W. Auchterlonie (17) with a brilliant 79 became the holder of the Championship Medal for one year, and received a golf charm, and fountain pen".

In April 1922 the Club bought Kinloch Cottage, standing on the corner of Links Place and North Street and next door to the Clubhouse. It cost £1570 and a Bazaar was organised as a means of raising funds. It was a major effort as this entry illustrates.

11th June 1923.

"In connection with the opening of the Bazaar, it was agreed to ask Mr. Boase to approach Sir Ralph Anstruther, Bart. to open the Bazaar on Thursday, 19th July, and

Sir Alex Sprot on Friday, 20th. Provost Sloan to open the Sale on Saturday and Baby Show at 3 o'clock. The time of opening was fixed as follows: Thursday 11.30 a.m., Friday, 2.30 p.m. & Saturday 1 p.m. Season Tickets 2/- each. Thursday from 11.30 to 4 p.m. 1/- - 6d afterwards; Friday 2.30 - 4 p.m. 1/- - 6d. afterwards; Saturday from 1 o'clock onwards 6d. Children under 12 half price.

It was decided to get the Glasgow Numerical Printing Coy. to print the admission tickets:

> 500 Season Tickets @ 2/- each
>
> 1000 Tickets @ 1/- each
>
> 3000 Tickets @ 6d each

and that special tickets be got for entertainments.

The Secretary was asked to consult Mr. J. Cargill Cantley, solicitor, as to whether or not we are entitled to pay entertainment Tax. Miss Johnstone, teacher, 1 City Road, arranged to give an entertainment by young children on Thursday from 3 to 4 and Saturday 5 to 6. A list of those who might be willing to assist with Bazaar was given in and it was arranged to have a meeting on Thursday, 21st inst. at 8.15 p.m. The ordinary Committee to meet at 7.30 p.m.

Mr. George Braid handed £6.13.3. to the Secretary, the result of Putting and Approaching Competitions during the winter months. Mr. R. Rutherford also handed the balance of £9.17.4, part of the sum realised from the airgun shooting competitions".

11th June 1923

"A sketch "Flag" (9ft. x 5ft.) was submitted with Club badge thereon - to cost 37/6 - it was decided to purchase same from Messrs. George Kenning & Son. It was decided to try and get the City Band to play on Thursday afternoon from 2 o'clock and also in the evening; the members of the band to be remunerated for their loss of time".

6th July 1923

"A letter was read from Mr. Cantley, Solicitor, that it was only necessary to pay entertainment Tax on the Side Shows (Concerts, etc.) for the Bazaar. It was decided that one shilling per head be allowed the City Silver Band and United Services Pipe Band for evening performances in lieu of refreshment at the Bazaar".

22nd August 1923

"It was agreed to take the following for Prizes from the six monthly Medal Competition from the surplus over Bazaar, e.g. Two drivers, two brassies, eight assorted iron clubs, four nickel plated walking sticks, nine golf balls, large box State Express cigarettes, 3 small boxes cigarettes, two razors, two tobacco pouches and one cigarette case".

11th December 1923

"Mr. H. Law reported that the Sub-Committee appointed to arrange a place for the Wireless set had met and that they suggested that the "Allan Robertson" (Captain's) box and one Club box on either side be removed and placed in the space where the Cup Case now sits, on the south side of the Reading Room, and that a small press be formed where the Club Boxes are removed. The Committee agreed to the suggestion and arranged for Messrs. Law & Sons carrying out the work".

18th November 1924

"It was agreed to hand over to St. Regulus Ladies Golf Club the Cot Quilt knitted by Queen Mary which had been part of the Bazaar surplus.

It was agreed to give a sum of £3 towards New Year's Prizes also a Club walking stick. It was decided to hold a Burns Concert in the Club similar to that held last year and a sum of £3 was allowed for expense of orchestra".

14th April 1925

"A letter was read from Mr. D. Blair, Match Secretary, stating that the Handicapping Committee were unanimous in holding an Annual Club Championship. The Conditions were:- the Competition to be open to all members of Club with sweepstake under handicap. The lowest 16 scratch scorers to play off under tournament Conditions. They also asked if the General Committee would be willing to provide 2 gold medals (one for winner and one for runner up) at a cost of approximately £4. annually. After discussion it was unanimously decided that one Championship badge be given at a cost of £2.10/-. The Committee also suggested that a 1/- sweepstake be held and that a percentage be laid aside towards making Competition self-supporting".

12th May 1925

"A deputation from the Handicapping Committee was present consisting of Messrs. Jas. Maloney, J.B. Melville and Tom Duncan. The deputation expressed the view that a Club Championship should be held and asked the General Committee to grant them a sum of £20 for this purpose. The Competition to be under somewhat similar lines to the Eden Tournament. Golf Badges to be provided for the Winner of the Championship and runner-up. Prizes to be played for under handicap and a special prize for the lowest scratch score".

18th May 1925

"A letter was read from Mr. D. Blair, Match Secretary, intimating that five members of the Handicapping Committee had resigned after the deputation which waited upon the General Committee had made their report. The declaration seemed rather strange no reply having been sent to the Handicapping Committee as to what action the General Committee intended taking with regard to Club Championship etc".

It was agreed to accept the resignation of those members of Handicapping Committee.

The Rustless Steel club provided by the Captain and Mr. Wm. McLaren for Competition among Visitor members of the Club was submitted to the Meeting and greatly admired by the members, it being an excellent piece of workmanship".

8th December 1925

"A letter was read from Mr. D. Blair suggesting that a portable electric heating appliance be fitted in Billiard Room. The Committee were of opinion that heating by electricity would be a costly matter and would not improve the heating of the Room. Gas heating was also suggested but after discussion it was decided to delay the matter in the meantime and instruct Club Steward to have fire lit by 5 o'clock each evening during the winter months.

The question of installing a telephone in Club was put before the meeting but the Committee considered it was not necessary".

19th January 1926

"It was intimated that 130 had been present at the Whist Drive, 128 actually playing. Refreshments cost 9d a head, which included cakes and sandwiches, the necessary dishes, and two women to take charge and do the washing up. Prizes being provided with the balance of the income. It was also agreed to place on record that the two large rooms were capable of holding 140 at such a function as above".

25th February 1926

"The Match Secretary's Report was a very satisfactory one. The high standard of play of former years had been maintained and in one instance exceeded where Mr. Lawrence Auchterlonie, the Veteran Club leader, returned a score of 68 over the Old Course creating a new record for Club competitions and also equalling the record held by George Duncan. Mr. Auchterlonie had an average of 77 for 13 rounds. Mr. Tom Duncan one of the younger school of players was a keen challenger for averages, being only a decimal point behind the leader".

14th June 1926

"The Committee approved of having Telephone in Club and agreed that it be placed in bar under control of the Club Steward and those using same stand at bottom of staircase. The Secretary was instructed to make enquiries regarding extension to Committee Room".

9th May 1927

"A letter was read from Mr. Gulley, Secretary, Royal and Ancient Club, enquiring if the St. Andrews Club would let them have the use of a writing room and lavatories for the Press at the time of the Open Championship and if so on what terms. It was agreed to grant the use of the Billiard Room for the Championship, also the lavatories, and that no charge be made".

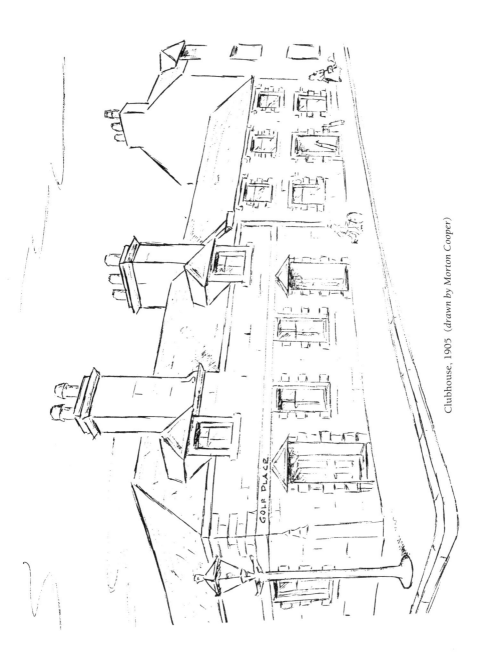

Clubhouse, 1905 (*drawn by Morton Cooper*)

12th September 1927

"Letters from Mr. Joshua Crayne were read to the Meeting intimating a gift of a set of golf clubs for competition among the members. The only conditions attached to the gift being that it should be a Bogey Competition under the Crayne System of Handicapping. Some discussion arose as to whether the Clubs should be played for as one prize or divided into several prizes. The Committee afterwards decided that it be divided into four prizes. The first 4 clubs, second 2 clubs, and 3rd and 4th each a club".

9th January 1928

"The Secretary was instructed to write the General Radio Coy. that unless the money paid for the wireless set was returned within one week, the matter would be placed in the hands of the Club's solicitor".

14th May 1928

"Electric Light. In view of the increased consumption Mr. W. Lamond was authorised to examine all the lamps in the Club and to report as to what alterations or reductions he considered advisable".

8th July 1929

"Old Cigarettes: The Secretary reported that certain brands of cigarettes had been in stock for over a year and he was asked to instruct the Match Secretary to purchase them for prizes for the August half yearly competition".

11th November 1929

"Steel Shafts: The Secretary pointed out that an article appeared in the November issue of "Golf Illustrated" stating that the St. Andrews Artisan Golf Club had authorised the use of steel shafts in their competition in opposition to the Rules of Golf as laid down by the Royal & Ancient Golf Club.

Silver Spoon: A letter was read from Miss Dorothy Lowry, Marinsulle, New Zealand, indicating that she understood St. Andrews presented a silver spoon to anyone doing a hole in one and as she had performed that feat, she made a request for the award. The novelty of the request appealed to the Committee and the Secretary was instructed to forward to the lady a silver spoon with the St. Andrews coat of arms, at the same time pointing out to her that she had been mis-informed".

3rd July 1930

"Singing: The Secretary was instructed to place a notice on the Notice Board to the effect that owing to complaints by neighbouring tenants no singing would be allowed in the Clubhouse after 10 p.m."

9th May 1932

"The Secretary was instructed to obtain a quotation from St. Leonards Laundry for the laundering of towels, etc. to obtain prices of Cash Registers and to inform the Steward that his use of firewood was excessive".

13th March 1933

"It was agreed to have Billiards, Domino and Draughts matches with the unemployed on Thursday. 23rd March".

15th June 1933

"A letter was read from Mr. Forgan indicating that he would not be able to house professionals during Championship period and asking if he would be in order to send them to the Club where they might keep their clubs, clothing etc.   It was agreed to accommodate the professionals in the Steward's Room which in the meantime would be left unpapered and unpainted.   The Secretary was instructed to ask Mr. Forgan if he could provide racks for clubs and to see if Mr. T. Kerr would be willing to undertake the duties of looking after the professionals' clubs, etc."

28th October 1933

"Mr. Boase explained that he had come to the meeting in his capacity as Chairman of the Advisory Council of the Unemployed Association to ask if the Committee would be willing to let part of Golf Place premises on a weekly basis at 10/- per week rental to that Association for recreation purposes for the unemployed.

Various details were discussed, chiefly concerning rates and taxes, cleaning and upkeep of the rooms, the keeping of good order, etc. and it was agreed to let the part of the old portion of the premises comprising Reading Room, Billiard Room and Lavatory accommodation, and the Captain, Vice Captain and Secretary were delegated to meet Mr. Boase and Mr. Cantley at 6 p.m. on Tuesday, 31st October, to draw up a missive of Let to be signed by the Secretary of the Association".

13th November 1933

"A letter was read from Mr. K. G...... complaining that he had not received his prize in the Half Yearly Competition nor the aggregate medal. The Secretary was instructed to remind Mr. G...... that his subscription for the current year had not been paid".

8th January 1934

"Mr. R. Baptie interviewed the Committee regarding the financing of a Book on the Club's history which might be published. He was asked to obtain information from Messrs. Innes as to probable cost, etc. and the Committee would consider thereafter what might be done in the matter.   Mr. Baptie expressed thanks for assistance rendered to him in his compilation of the Club's history and intimated he would like to give a second lecture which was fixed for 8 p.m. on Tuesday, 23rd January".

12th February 1934

"Sketches of a suggested Club Tie were submitted from Messrs. J.C. Smith and

The formal clubhouse opening was held on 20th July 1933. The property was bought for £2,700.
The Chapter "Our Clubhouses" gives the details. (drawn by Morton Cooper)

drawing No. 1428 was accepted on the understanding that the Club was in no way responsible for the sale of such ties".

8th March 1934

"The Match Secretary's report indicated that 1933 had been one of the most successful years in the history of the Club so far as golf was concerned. The lowest nett score had been 64 and 70 had been broken on numerous occasions. The entries for the various Competitions and Tournaments had been larger than ever and the younger members had been well to the front in most of the events. The Club Championship was won by Mr. L.B. Ayton, Jnr. at his first attempt, and Mr. A.B. Taylor, our youngest member now, had won the Boys Championship for the second successive year. Mr. A. Rolland had won the Tait Medal and the Club had been successful in the annual encounters with Carnoustie and Leven".

14th October 1934

"The question of card playing in the Club was on Agenda. After general discussion it was decided that play might be in Bar Lounge on inner side of sliding door, when this was drawn over.

No play to be allowed in the open lounge, and members wishing then to play were to be referred to the spare room opposite the Committee Room. No Sunday play".

9th July 1934

"Resignations of two or three members owing to unemployment were intimated".

12th November 1934

"The Scroll Book containing Mr. R. Baptie's "Ninety Years of Golf" was on the table. This contains a full history of St. Andrews Golf Club, and will be valuable for reference purposes. On the motion of Mr. J.F. Auchterlonie, seconded by Mr. A.F. Duncan it was decided to give Mr. Baptie a cheque for £3.3.0. to mark the Club's appreciation of his work in compiling the statistics".

10th December 1934

"St. Regulus. Secretary was instructed to write and thank Miss Wilson for the use of their Piano for our Smoker, and to send a present of an umbrella as a prize for their next competition".

15th October 1935

"It was reported that Messrs. Younger's Head Brewer had called, and after conversation with Captain, Vice-Captain and Secretary, had proposed sending one of their staff to see if the cause of the complaints could be found. They did so, and the man worked with the Steward for 2/3 days. The routine of the draughting process by the Steward left nothing for complaint, but certain fittings were faulty and have now been replaced".

13th January 1936

"The suggestion to play Pyramids or Snooker was not agreed to".

23rd January 1936

"The meeting had been called in connection with letter received that day from Town Council inviting the Members of the Club to be present at the King's Proclamation the following day. It was arranged that as many members as possible would walk from the Club at 2.30 p.m."

Annual Report for 1935

"We regret to record the death of ... Mr. David Leitch. Mr. Leitch was a past Captain of the Club and although past man's allotted span, maintained his interest in the game to the last, winning our Haig Cup as recently as 1932.

In the "Golfer" in 1896 he was described as "One of the prettiest players who ever handled a Club", and his style as one of the easy graceful styles that last a lifetime.

He took part in the "Amateur" as far back as 1888, and reached the Semi-Final at Hoylake in 1890, and was one of seven players to represent the Club in 1895. He was a winner of the "Evening Times" Trophy, and Runner-up for the "Telegraph" Cup".

14th May 1936

"Complaints were made that cycles were parked in Club entrance, and also in front of rails, instead of being placed in Area Cycle Racks. Secretary instructed to get a Notice Board".

8th June 1936

"Letters from Secretary of Barry, Ostler and Nairn's Golf Club asking courtesy of Club for Saturday, 13th June. and also Messrs. Stewart, Cleek-workers for their match with Kingsbarns on Saturday 27th June, were agreed to".

18th August 1936

"Mr. L.B. Ayton made a suggestion that he would be pleased to give instruction to those members desirous of it, if the Committee would arrange to make suitable accommodation for same. Mr. Ayton was thanked for his offer, and it was agreed to ascertain to what extent other professionals in the Club would assist in the matter".

31st August 1936

"The question of Golf Practice or Tuition for members of the Club during the winter was fully discussed. In regard to the use of a Net, the opinion was that there was no suitable place in the Club for such practice. To consider the Reading Room for this was open to objection on the grounds of probable damage to property, a likelihood of complaints of noise from adjoining tenants. In regard to question of costs, from quotations received, a suitable Net and Mat would cost from £15-£22. The Secretary was instructed to enquire of the Professionals in the Club whether they would be willing to co-operate, and report to a further meeting".

10th March 1938

"The Secretary reported that Mr. Ayton had informed him that the P.G.A. were unable to quote us for Golf Practice Nets.

Prices for Nets from Edwards, West Bridport (per Jack Barnett and Tom Morris), Lumleys, Glasgow, and B.S. Spalding & Bros. Ltd. London, were before the meeting.

After discussion it was unanimously agreed to recommend to the General Committee that it was inadvisable to purchase a Net, which would cost at a minimum £16-20, and for which there is not suitable accommodation without an annexe to the premises being provided.

It was suggested that the Professionals might agree to give Practice Lectures on the art of golf, with demonstrations. Carpet Bowls to be suspended upon the nights arranged for the lectures.

The following members were elected to Life Membership:

      Laurence Auchterlonie

      Walter Anderson

In submitting the names to the meeting the Captain said that Mr. Auchterlonie was one of our oldest and best known members, winner of the American Open in 1902 and the Western Open".

11th April 1938

"Permission was granted for use of Card Room on 2nd, 3rd, and 4th June for Teleprinter in connection with Walker Cup Competition. Fee as before".

16th April 1938

"Mr. Wilson raised the question of the proposed alterations to the Eden Course and stated that he found very general criticism and objections to certain of the proposals. There was general discussion, in which the Captain and L.B. Ayton took part, and as there was agreement with Mr. Wilson's remarks, he moved that the Town Council be asked to receive a deputation from the Club on the matter. This was agreed on".

14th August 1938

"Mr. J.H. Thompson made a complaint regarding quality of, or condition in which beer was served, and was supported by Mr. P.W. Hutton. Secretary in reply maintained that there were no reasonable grounds for complaint, as the Steward gave the draughting of the beer every care and attention, and outside a very limited number of our members, who over his period as Secretary made a practice of complaining, there had been no complaints which called for investigation".

9th January 1939

"Secretary intimated that Mr. Gullen had enquired regarding accommodation for players in Open Championship. It was agreed to give all players courtesy of Club, and arrange for care of clubs as in 1933".

1st March 1939

"The Secretary suggested that the feelings of the members might be ascertained at the Annual Meeting in regard to ear-marking a sum each year to meet the expenses that would be incurred in having a fitting celebration at the Club's Centenary".

9th March 1939

"Mr. J.C. Ramsay made reference to anticipated celebrations of the centenary of the Club in 1943. These would require to be in keeping with the high place which the Club held in the history of golf, and the Committee suggested that if the accounts of the Club continued in the same favourable condition, a certain sum or sums might be ear-marked each following year as a contribution to the expenses, and in order that all members might be able to participate. This was seconded by Mr. D. Carstairs, and agreed to".

10th July 1939

"Secretary read letter from Secretary of Midlands Association thanking Club for use of Club, and also for the prize given, and a letter from Commander Roe of the P.G.A. thanking Club for the privileges extended to their members during the period of the Open".

10th July 1939

"The Open. Before proceeding with the business of the meeting the Captain made complimentary reference to the creditable position taken by three of the Club members in this Tournament, and Secretary was instructed to write Messrs. L.B. Ayton, L.B. Ayton, Jnr. and Andrew Dowie, conveying the good wishes of the Committee and member".

The Minutes of the Club covering the First World War make little mention of the conflict and its effect on our members. The Second World War does get regular mention.

The first death of a serving member is duly recorded. This occurred during the retreat to Dunkirk while he was serving in the 1st Fife and Forfar Yeomanry. Thereafter other deaths of members are detailed.

The Club kept in touch with its members sending regular Postal Orders to all parts of the world.

12th November 1939

"It was arranged to keep the following medals in the safe during the war: Scratch and Handicap Medals, Aggregate, Monthly, R & A, F.G. Tait, Boys' Championship and Captain's Chain".

January 1940

"The Captain at the close of the meeting handed over a genuine Hugh Philp Club, for which he was suitably thanked. It was agreed to have this suitably placed in Trophy Case".

10th June 1940

"Mr. Philp raised the question of the Club's records. After discussion it was arranged that they be stored in cupboard in basement. Mr. Law to supply any packages required, and strengthen door".

8th July 1940

"Secretary reported that he had now obtained the present addresses of those members who were serving in H.M. Forces, and read draft copy of letter to be sent to these members enclosing a Postal Order for 5/-".

9th September 1940

"Letter from Town Clerk was read handing to custody of Club the Duke of York's Cup, also the Victory Cup, won in the recent Eden Tournament by Mr. A.T. Soutar. Mr. Cantley intimated that both cups were fully insured.

Secretary had informed Mr. Cantley that we would store them with our other Trophies and Medals in basement, of which the following are particulars:-

Cups	Medals
Kyle Cup	Spring Scratch
Jubilee Cup	" Handicap
Hugon Cup	Autumn Handicap
Guy Campbell	" Scratch
Jock Hutchison	Aggregate
Seniors (J. Macdonalds)	Monthly
Coronation (Jas Stewart)	Boys' Championship
Charles Grieve	Tait (property of Tait
Haig	Medal Committee)
Junior	Captains' Medal
McGregor Trophy	─────────
United Services & Medal	
(property of St. Andrews	Visitors' Trophy (Putter)
United Services Association)	Hugh Philp Spoon (1819)
Rolland Cup	Feather Ball "
(Boys' Championship)	

10th November 1940

"A letter was read from Mr. W. Fowlis asking for use of two of the Club's Air Guns, for the Post Office Home Guard. This was granted".

8th December 1940

"The guns lent to Post Office Home Guard had been returned, as they were found defective.

Secretary reported that over 100 members were now away, and that amount of Comforts Fund was not sufficient to send 5/- to each member. It was agreed to make P.O. 4/-.

It was decided to print Fixture Card with all competitions omitting Club Championships.

Mr. J.F. Auchterlonie handed in at the meeting 3 Old Feather Golf Balls, which he had received from Miss Bruce, Market St., St. Andrews, as a gift to the Club. These had been the property of her father, the late well known Mr. George Bruce, who was an early member of the Club, joining it in 1847, and was Secretary in 1852 and Captain 1855/1856.

One of the balls bears date 1772 and maker unknown. Another was made by Allan Robertson, and dated 1844. The other is a much larger ball and dated perhaps 1779, and Peter Thomson, St. Andrews, as maker.

Secretary was instructed to write and thank Miss Bruce for her thoughtful gift, which would be highly appreciated by the Club. On the motion of Mr. Hutton, Mr. Auchterlonie was thanked for his interest in the matter".

13th March 1941

"Mr. Blair enquired regarding the provison being made for the Centenary Fund, and if any definite figure was aimed at.

The Captain stated that with the eminence held by the Club as the premier Artisan Club considerable entertaining would require to be done on the occasion, and for the Company we might have as guests it would require to be done in a fitting manner, and it would at the same time be necessary that the price of the tickets for the anticipated function be at a figure that all our members could be present if they wished. For one thing part of the fund would cover any loss on price of tickets.

Membership. Annual Report for 1940.

Subscriptions paid were 493 and adding those members who in H.M. Forces were exempted from payment of subscription the membership at end of year was 566, against a total of 614 for the previous year. The reduction of 48 in membership is mainly due to a fall of 35 in our Country Members, so our local membership has been well maintained in the present circumstances. Temporary Members were only 42 against 168 for 1939, but we hope that St. Andrews may have a better season this summer than was unfortunately the case last year, and that this important item in our revenue may benefit".

13th April 1941

"Mr. P.W. Hutton offered a Wire Haired Terrier as prize for a Draw in aid of Members War Comforts Fund.   It was decided to put 2 x 100 ticket books on sale in Club".

12th May 1941

"The Captain informed the meeting that an official of the Air Ministry, with R.A.F. Officer, had inspected the premises on Friday last, and in case of any development in commandeering the premises for Military purposes, the Captain, with Messrs. J.F. Auchterlonie and W. Lamond, were appointed an Emergency Committee, with powers".

25th June 1941

"The question of a reduced payment for the members of the New Club now joining was raised, and after discussion it was moved by Mr. J.F. Auchterlonie, and seconded by Mr. A. Ramsay that for the period to end of 1941 the charge be 10/-, with entry fee of 5/-.

An amendment that the ordinary rates be charged was moved by Mr. W. Lamond and seconded by Mr. H. Campbell.   On a vote the amendment was carried.

On account of the increased numbers in the bar in the evening the Secretary was authorised to get assistance for two hours each evening meantime".

4th August 1941

"The meeting had been called to consider some restriction on the sales of Whisky and Wines.   The Secretary reported that the Bar figures for July exceeded £500 and that the total for the 7 months practically equalled the total for whole of 1940.

The considerable stock of Whisky which we had on hand at beginning of year was now much reduced, and our 50% ration worked out at only 4 cases per month".

12 October 1941

"The question of Carpet Bowls was raised.   Taking into consideration the large numbers that were now often in the Bar Lounge, preventing the use of the front portion as a Reading Room, and more particularly the imminence of requisitioning by the authorities, it was not considered advisable to lay the carpet this season".

9th November 1941

"Secretary explained present position of stocks, and how affected by present rate of rationing.   On the suggestion of Mr. Lamond, it was arranged to further restrict the supply of spirits, and decided that there be no sales of Whisky on Mondays and Wednesdays as from Monday, 17th November.   There was a complaint by Mr.

103

Hutton that spirit sales were still taking place after 9.30 p.m."

14th December 1941

"Secretary reported that membership at end of year was 582, of these 501 were local and 81 country members. There were 121 of above total exempted from payment of subscription during 1941, as serving in one of H.M. Forces. To date 148 of our members were serving in H.M. Forces since outbreak of war".

11th January 1942

"Secretary presented Income & Expenditure Accounts with Draft Balance sheet for 1941. The year closed with a surplus of £609.18.1 against a figure of £173.12.9. for 1940.

The net income at £1609.5.8. showed an increase of £548.16.7. Expenditure at £1002.2.7. was an increase of £105.6.3. made up of larger amounts for Salaries and Assistance, War Damage Insurance, and Laundry and Cleaning.

The Captain gave an analysis of the figures, and said that the Club was really in a marvellously good financial position. The liquid assets, Cash, Investments, & Stock were almost equal to amount of balance of bond outstanding, and considerably over adding Centenary Fund. This meant that Club Premises & Contents were free of any liability. Results partly due to use of Club by R.A.F."

13th December 1942

"The Secretary reported on the supplies of Wines & Spirits at date, and it was arranged that a certain limited quantity might be sold in bottles or half bottles between 21st December and 2nd January inclusive. Prices to be as follows:-

      Whisky Bottle 23/-   Half bottle 12/-

      Port & Sherry Bottle 15/-   "   "   7/6

As there was a good stock of gin, members could get a bottle of this at 22/6.

Owing to tightening of supplies by various of our traders, the quantity due each month would be at least 3/4 cases less than last year.

The following restrictions were agreed to:-

1. No wines or spirits to be sold at any time on Tuesdays and Fridays.

2. On other days, including Saturdays, no wines or spirits to be served after 9 p.m.

3. All sales to be confined to 'Nips' - no glasses to be served.

4. In the meantime, these restrictions do not apply to the sale of Gin.

5. To come into force on Monday, 15th March".

11th March 1943 at A.G.M.

"Before calling on the Secretary to read the Minutes of last A.G.M., the Captain intimated that the following telegram had been received from Mr. Philp, at Gibraltar.

"Heartiest congratulations centenary,

Kindest regards, David Philp"

The Captain in moving the adoption of the Report and Statement of Accounts, referred to several items on the Balance Sheet, particularly the allocation to the Centenary Fund, the occasion of which, our Centenary this year (1943), required to be put off until later, when it would be a Centenary and Victory function, the allocation of £35 to our Members War Comforts Fund, and also the sum of £300 to Club Premises Improvements Fund".

And so the Club reached its Centenary year in a world concerned with much more serious matters than golf. Over 200 members served in the armed forces. Around twenty of them were serving in the Fife and Forfar Yeomanry and training for the D Day landings in Normandy the following year. Those left in the town had heavy commitments contributing to the war effort on the home front. No doubt all our golf enthusiasts tried to find time to hit an occasional ball about despite the many wartime difficulties.

OUR CLUB HOUSES

By the 1890's, St. Andrews Golf Club was very powerful in the golf world but it still had to meet in various hotels in the town. Our members obviously realised that only the purchase of a Club house would establish the Club firmly and permanently. A variety of Minutes show our Committees taking the matter very seriously. I have recorded the various negotiations at some length because they reflect the tenacity of our members. Without its own Club house, it is almost certain that the St. Andrews Golf Club would have slowly declined and disappeared as did most of the other 19th century clubs in the town.

23rd May 1895

"The necessity of acquiring a Club house was discussed and Messrs. R.B. Stewart, A. Milne and Jas. Stewart were appointed a deputation to wait upon Mr. Rusack with a view to ascertain if a piece of ground below the Hotel could be got for a site."

20th August 1985

"The Club house question was again discussed and it was decided to make enquiries regarding the "Gate House" in Golf Place."

21st December 1896

"The Secretary read a letter from Mr. Jas. Kirk intimating his refusal to sell part of his property in Pilmuir Links for the Club to erect a Club house."

12th March 1898

"The Captain then intimated to the Committee that he had written a letter to Mr. Cheape, Strathtyrum, stating that the Club wished to acquire a piece of his property on which to build a Club House. Honeyman's Garden* was mentioned as a place that would suit the requirements of the Club and also that he afterwards held a conversation with Mr. Cheape who expressed himself as favourable to the scheme and mentioned that the said piece of ground was very valuable, and also that he would like to see a sketch of a Club House the Club would erect thereon. Through the trouble taken by Mr. Anderson, Architect, about the form of the garden and the drainage levels there and he having informed the Captain about the same (knowing the Club wanted that ground) such information the Captain found was of much service to the Club in his conversation with Mr. Cheape."

"After discussion it was resolved to call a General Meeting of the Club for Tuesday, 22nd inst. to sanction the necessary arrangements for getting a plan drawn to lay before Mr. Cheape and to further the scheme of a Club House in the best possible manner."

17th June 1898

"The Captain then on behalf of the Special Club House Committee made a statement showing the result of their negotiations with Mr. Anderson, Architect and afterwards with Mr. Cheape, Strathtyrum, about procuring a site for a Club House and drawing plans for same.

"Mr. Anderson had drawn several plans and submitted them to Mr. Cheape, one of which was approved. He likewise had offered a certain sum of money as Feu Duty which also had been considered satisfactory."

"The Captain afterwards had a conference with Mr. Cheape and his Agent, Mr. Grace, in the latter's office when Mr. Cheape said that the St. Andrews Club would get the ground on the condition that in future the members of the Club be restricted to people belonging to and residing in St. Andrews."

"The Captain was much surprised at this condition and strongly objected to the Club restricting its membership by any such agreement but promised to lay Mr. Cheape's views before a General Meeting of the Club and let him know the results. A discussion then followed the Captain's statement on behalf of the Committee and the unanimous voice of the members present was not take the ground on the terms proposed by Mr. Cheape and his Agent."

"A. Milne moved and Jas. Robb seconded the following motion 'That the special Club House Committee be discharged, the meeting according them a vote of thanks for the efforts they had made to secure a site for a Club House, the Committee of Management to carry on further negotiations with Mr. Cheape but not to agree to any stipulations restricting the future membership of the Club only to those belonging to or resident in St. Andrews and that they also endeavour to secure any other ground or premises they may think suitable for a Club House no bargain or contract to be binding on the Club before being subject to a General Meeting.'"

* [Honeyman's Garden was the name given to the ground behind the 17th green. It is an interesting thought that without Mr. Cheape's last minute change of mind, the St. Andrews Golf Club members might have spent the next century looking down on all the many Road Hole dramas from their Club House Lounge. However, we would not have been able to view all the 18th hole dramas.]

25th February 1899

"A discussion took place on the subject of whether it was practicable for the Club to erect a shelter on the Links similar to the shelter erected by the Ladies Golf Club on their green and subject to the same regulations and conditions and also to bear the same relation between its members and the public in its management especially as regards its internal privacy. The opinion was unanimous that such a shelter would have to be in close proximity to the first tee and that it would be desirable to write to the Town Council to ascertain if they would grant the Club permission to erect such a shelter before incurring any expenses for plans or otherwise."

"The Captain and Secretary were appointed to approach Baillie Balsillie to ascertain if his property abutting on the Links could be rented or leased by the Club for the use of its members as a Club House and to report at the next meeting."

11th February 1901

"There was a large attendance of members .... The Captain stated 'That the meeting had more particularly been called for to enable the members to discuss the appointment of a Special Committee for the purpose of acquiring Mr. Kirk's property at Pilmuir Links, which is to be sold on 19th inst., for a Club House."

The property was purchased for considerably more than our Committee was prepared to offer.

29th August 1903

"It was proposed to approach the Liberal and A.O.F. Golf Club to co-operate with the St. Andrews Club to ask the Town Council to grant a site to build a Club House on the Bruce Embankment. To be an Artisan Club named St. Andrews Golf Club."

4th September 1903

"Committee to meet the delegates of Liberal and A.O.F.Golf Club on above date at Liberal Rooms. R. Wallace, Chairman. The two Clubs pledged themselves to help the St. Andrews Club to get a site. It was carried that a letter be sent to Town Clerk for first meeting of council asking them to consider the question and if they would meet the Clubs on the question."

2nd March 1905

"The Property Committee met on this date to consider the advisability of acquiring a property in Kirk Place as a Club House. It was resolved to recommend the Club to bid for the house occupied by Mrs. Smith, and Messrs. Strath and Robertson were appointed as Sub Committee to ascertain what money the members and friends would generate at the rate of 5%; and to report to the Secretary when a meeting of the Club would be called."

14th March 1905

"The Secretary then explained the action of the Property Committee in recommending the purchase of the house in Kirk Place and introduced the question of the guarantee fund.

Mr. Robertson then reported the progress made in collecting the necessary funds, and showed a rough plan procured for the information of the Committee. After considerable discussion as to alterations and prospects of the scheme, the Secretary

Our members were always ready to lend money to the Club both in 1905 and 1932 when it was required to fund the new clubhouses.

109

The Building Committee which organised our first clubhouse in 1905 in what is now Auchterlonie's Shop
.Standing : Walter Anderson, Robert Robertson, A. Schimm, Angus McGregor, (succeeded A. Strath),
Seated : A. Dewar, Alex Milne, George Greig (Captain), Thomas Stuart and David Auchterlonie

1932 Links House Committee

stated that he was indebted to Mr. Schimm for much valuable information as to the probable cost and profits of such an undertaking.

Mr. Schimm then explained his scheme in detail showing that a considerable profit was likely to result if carried out on good lines. After further discussion, Mr. Schimm proposed that the Committee be informed to buy the property. Mr. Robertson urged that an effort be made to acquire the property and Mr. Greig suggested that a Committee be appointed to buy the house. Mr. Wilson moved that a Committee of 3 or 5 be appointed. Mr. Schimm seconded 5 which was carried. This Committee to co-operate with the Property. Mr. Walter Anderson suggested that the Committee buy any of the three houses for sale. Messrs. Greig, Schimm, D. Auchterlonie, A. Robertson and A. Strath were then appointed with the Secretary."

13th April 1905

"The Chairman called upon M Cargill Cantley who was present to give the meeting some information with regard to the financial position. Mr. Cantley stated that they could raise a loan of £600 on the property of 4 per cent and with £530 guaranteed they had £330 in hand for alterations, furnishings etc. He gave a simple explanation of what had to be done in the way of appointing trustees and granting a bond."

Our first Clubhouse was bought for £800. Immediately a host of minor problems had to be considered and resolved. For example:

5th October 1905

"Draught Beer. The Secretary was instructed to order Draught from Messrs. Youngers & Coy, Edinburgh, same as supplied to the R&A Club.

Shooting Amusement. On the question of Mr. R. Wallace it was agreed to recommend to the General Committee the purchase of two airguns + Targets, making a small charge for the use of same, and that a sub committee be appointed to carry out the arrangements."

6th November 1906

"Cycle House. It was to ask Mr. David Craig to put up a temporary erection at the back of the Club House with a corrugated iron roof for the accommodation of cycles."

3rd May 1907

"The minutes of the meeting of the committee held on 1st ult. and 2nd inst. were read and approved.

Gas Fittings. The Committee decided to adopt gas for the new building and it was stated that Mr. Hall, gas manager, had offered to fit up 18 lights throughout the Club House at a cost of 22/6 yearly for seven years, payable quarterly and at the end of that period the gas fittings would become the property of the Club."

4th June 1907

"The minutes of the meeting of the committee held on 7th ult. were read and

The Bar Lounge in 1946.
Our present bar is now where the two windows are, the bar then was the hatch in the wall.

The Bar Lounge in 1992.
The doorway in the 1946 picture was blocked off.

approved of.

Supply of Liquor - Samples of whisky from the firms of Messrs. Walker & Sons and McIntosh & McIntosh were tested by the committee and the committee resolved to order a "Special" Blend Walker & Sons at 14/10 besides having the blend at present on sale.

Bazaar Surplus. The committee agreed, on condition that Mr. Singer relinquish a sum of £3 which he claims as due to him from the Bazaar Funds, that he be allowed to take the Japanese Umbrellas. It was stated that a case of two dozen Whisky should be taken into stock."

In 1922 when the property next door came on the market the club decided to go for expansion. This was the corner property now part of Auchterlonie's shop. It cost £1,575.

23rd May 1922.

"It was decided not to advertise the Kitchen portion of Kinloch Cottage which the Club did not intend to occupy at present. Several applications had been made for these rooms and after consideration it was decided to offer the St. Regulus Ladies' Club the premises at an annual rent of (£15)."

Early in 1932, the committee had drawn up plans to develop our buildings but these were cancelled "in view of the financial crisis through which the country had been passing".

Suddenly in August, however, the minutes show us that the committee had bought Links House, our present home, for £2700 without consulting the members. My information is that the Club had prior knowledge that the property was coming on the market and moved within days to buy it secretly before its availability was known in the town. It was a case of "Cometh the hour, Cometh the committee". We can only be grateful that they had the nerve to act so positively and swiftly and hand us the present Club house with its superb setting looking onto the Old Course's 18th green.

8th August 1932

"The Captain explained to the meeting that the General Committee had purchased the Links House for the sum of £2700 and that the purpose of the meeting was to get the Trustees to homologate that action. Mr. Cantley gave a very lucid explanation regarding the negotiations for the property especially as to the reason for not calling a general meeting of the members beforehand.

The draft plan of the property was submitted and the treasurer gave an account of the financial position of the Club showing that the actual assets (after deducting liabilities for debentures) were £1200 cash plus the value of the present property. The president and Mr. Provan expressed themselves as fully approving the General Committee's action, of the Links House as an ideal site for a club house and also

The Reading and Luncheon Room in 1946. This is now the Middle Lounge.
Its bar is where the windows were in this photograph.

commended the Club on its financial position. The action of the committee was therefore entirely homologated. The Captain thanked the President, the Trustees and Mr. Cantley for their kindness and the secretary was instructed to call an Extraordinary general meeting of the members at 8 p.m. on Thursday 25th August."

25th August 1932

"The Captain explained to the meeting the various steps the Committee had taken in purchasing the Links House for the sum of £2700, especially stressing the fact that the renovation of the present property was to cost in excess of £4000."

The conversion of a large Victorian house into a golf club house presented problems and the necessary alterations costing £2000 were authorised. It was decided to borrow £1000 at 4% from club members in multiples of £25. The two properties forming our first clubhouse were sold for £1800.

17th July 1933

"It was intimated by the Captain that the formal opening of the Club's new premises had been arranged for Thursday 20th July at 8.30 p.m. and the secretary was instructed to have invitations sent to representatives of all local golf clubs, Leven and Carnoustie clubs, contractors, architects and Mr. Cantley and the Vice President. It was stated Provost Boase had made a gift of a Barrel of Beer for the occasion and the Captain intimated that he and the Vice Captain had purchased a cigarette box specially inscribed for £3.5.6 to present to the Provost as a momento of the occasion.

The Secretary was authorised to obtain 6 enamel cups for the serving of beer during the evening and to place a supply of brandy, whisky, soda at the head of the table."

Just before the outbreak of war, plans were drawn up to cover over what had been the cycle basement outside our present entrance but these were shelved and brought out again in 1945. For years building restrictions made it very difficult to carry out even internal improvements.

At the 1970 A.G.M. a plan was put forward to develop the Upper Lounge. This involved removing part of the rear wall and building a new bar and store on top of the lower bar and store, and replacing the Reading Room wall with a sliding partition to create the L-shaped room. Despite opposition, the plan was approved and implemented, giving the members much needed additional space.

The final part of the clubhouse story was put in place when in 1977 our committee purchased the basement of the next door property which was converted into the Mixed Lounge we know. Support has been "mixed" but whatever its future, it represents a very valuable addition to the assets of the Club.

Future developments of the building are difficult to anticipate. If the pressure on space increases, it may be possible to extend our building at the rear. Alternatively, it might be possible to fill in the central well though this would require extensive and expensive internal alterations. We have an imperfect building on the perfect site.

The Middle Lounge, 1993

JUST A MINUTE III

(1944-1993)

The third fifty years of the Club have seen a slow and steady but unspectacular growth. The purchase of our first clubhouse in 1905 was the turning point in our development. Without a home of its own St. Andrews Golf Club might well have faded away after the First World War. With its own property and canny but far sighted committees it has prospered - both financially and as a golf club.

Obviously we will never recapture the glory days of last century when we could produce Allan Robertson, the two Morrises, Andrew Strath, Tom Kidd, Bob Martin, Jamie Anderson, and Willie Fernie. The St. Andrews Golf Club was right at the heart of the early development of the modern world of golf which we take for granted.

These years have seen a steady succession of very talented club players, some of whom have made their mark nationally as amateurs and professionals.

Our club house was a busy place during the Second World War. Although our younger members were away in the Services, other army and airforce personnel stationed in the area were regular visitors.

Picture of Dinner

116

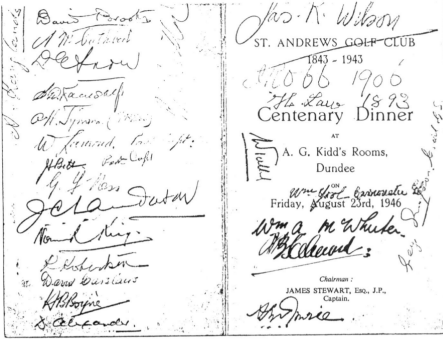

ST. ANDREWS GOLF CLUB

1843 - 1943

Centenary Dinner

AT

A. G. Kidd's Rooms,
Dundee

ON
Friday, August 23rd, 1946

Chairman :
JAMES STEWART, Esq., J.P.,
Captain.

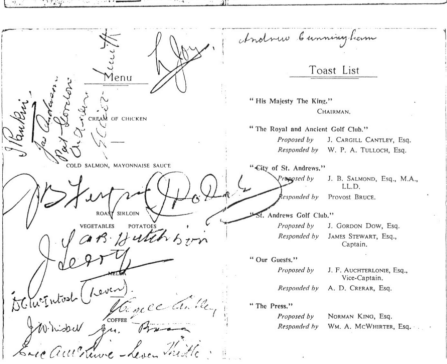

Menu

CREAM OF CHICKEN

COLD SALMON, MAYONNAISE SAUCE

ROAST SIRLOIN

VEGETABLES   POTATOES

MELBA

COFFEE

Toast List

"His Majesty The King."
          CHAIRMAN.

"The Royal and Ancient Golf Club."
    Proposed by   J. CARGILL CANTLEY, Esq.
    Responded by   W. P. A. TULLOCH, Esq.

"City of St. Andrews."
    Proposed by   J. B. SALMOND, Esq., M.A.,
                   LL.D.
    Responded by   Provost BRUCE.

"St. Andrews Golf Club."
    Proposed by   J. GORDON DOW, Esq.
    Responded by   JAMES STEWART, Esq.,
                   Captain.

"Our Guests."
    Proposed by   J. F. AUCHTERLONIE, Esq.,
                   Vice-Captain.
    Responded by   A. D. CRERAR, Esq.

"The Press."
    Proposed by   NORMAN KING, Esq.
    Responded by   WM. A. McWHIRTER, Esq.

117

Already our committee had decided that the Centenary celebrations would be combined with the Victory celebration after the end of the war and funds had been built up to pay for this.

Various venues were considered for the Centenary Dance - the Town Hall, the Younger Hall - even the Drill Hall - but all were rejected. It was decided that it should be held in the premises of A.G. Kidd in Dundee and this required us to hire a special train to take members across the Tay.

Four hundred members took part - a very large gathering to arrange in a time of stringent food rationing. They sat down to a six-course dinner costing 15/- per head (7/6d to members)

In addition our finances were strong enough to allow us to consider paying off the Bonds which members had taken out to finance the purchase of the present club house.

Sadly our stocks of beer and whisky were less secure. Allocations of both were cut and generated friction. Some members complained about the discourteous attitude of the Steward. Our Secretary shrewdly pointed out that "from his knowledge the scarcity of whisky was a prime factor in such a matter, and it must be remembered that we were all labouring under what had been five or six years excessive labour or efforts."

As World War II ended another war broke out between the local golfers and the Town Council which had the temerity to issue a Provisional Order requiring that local golfers be charged for their golf. Immediately the Club asked the Town Council to receive a deputation to discuss this. After a first refusal the two sides met but without reaching any agreement.

By April the Committee had sought legal advice and our lawyer was asked to seek Counsel's opinion. One fact to be established from this was that any objections to the Provisional Order could only be made by individual Municipal Voters, not the Golf Club.

There was an Extraordinary General Meeting called in May 1946 to discuss the situation. Not surprisingly, some 250 members crowded in to make their views known. One sobering fact given was that pursuing the dispute in the Courts might well cost £350-£500 - a very substantial sum at that time. (Our total subscriptions came to less that £500). Small wonder that the Club backed off.

There were light-hearted times in the Club in the immediate post-war years. The annual match with Carnoustie was a highlight of our golfing year. The postcards inviting members to play in the team were highly prized.

The road bridge was not built and the Tay had to be crossed by ferry. There are stories of J.K. Wilson strumming his mandolin on the boat while team mates tap danced, and fired golf balls off the deck into the water. Regularly the last ferry was missed and the bus had to come home via Perth.

Our first ever club match was with Leven in 1849 and the first of many matches with Carnoustie Golf Club was played in 1873. Thereafter games were played against our two old rivals intermittently. In 1953 the Lindsay Shield was presented as a trophy for competition in a three sided fixture involving the St. Andrews Golf Club, Leven Thistle and Carnoustie Golf Club. Teams of fifty aside - twenty five playing at home, twenty five away from home - compete annually in the Spring. Currently the St. Andrews team will be made up mostly of players with handicap 7 and under. "Unique" is a word which is badly misused but surely this fixture must be unique in inter club golf ?

It was J.K. Wilson who was responsible for the St. Andrews Golf Club featuring in the national press in May 1950. The British Amateur Championship was held that year on the Old Course and J.K. was drawn to play Harry L. Crosby in the first round. At that time Bing Crosby had an enormous following both as a singer and as a film star, and around 3000 spectators saw the two play off. Bing Crosby had a handicap of 2 and started off 3,3,4 to be three up but thereafter his game fell apart and the match ended at the 16th green in heavy rain with J.K. the winner.

The two men kept in touch thereafter and later on, in 1972, Bing Crosby agreed to a suggestion to put up a trophy to be played for by Senior Golfers. This is enthusiastically supported each Autumn by the golden oldies of the town's male golf clubs.

The years immediately following the War were not easy ones for the Club. Although we had money to spend on improving our building, it was difficult to obtain the Building Permits needed to carry out the necessary work.

The minutes of these fifty years are full of the trivia which occupy much of a Committee's time but which have to be dealt with to keep any Golf Club functioning.

At the A.G.M. of 1952 it was proposed that the subscription be raised from 15/- to £1 but this was voted down by the members.

The A.G.M. of 1954 saw an argument about whether the Club should purchase a TV set. This in turn provoked another argument as to whether a motion from the floor which was carried by a majority was binding on the Management Committee. Legal opinion was sought and the ruling was given that a Committee was responsible for organising all the business of a golf club independent of A.G.M. decisions. Eventually a TV set was installed. This in turn aroused more controversy between those wishing to view and those wanting peace and quiet.

Whisky supplies were always a matter for discussion. In 1952 proprietary whisky was only on sale three nights a week. One entry reads:

"The Secretary stressed the fact that during the past three months we had received 126 bottles of whisky whereas we had sold 206 bottles. He quoted figures to show

Old Course, waiting on 4th tee
(British Amateur 1950)

that if we continued at the present rate.... we would have very little proprietary whisky left at the end of the year." It would seem that all kinds of dubious non-proprietary whiskies were around, e.g.

"It was agreed to get rid of the five remaining bottles of Australian whisky by means of raffles and as prizes on New Year's Day."

1958 saw the start of another dispute, which still rumbles on - that with the Scottish Golf Union, which was looking for 1/- subscription per member. Not for the first time the Club seriously considered withdrawing from the S.G.U. but drew back from this because of the complication it would create for individual members and other clubs in Fife. Many club golfers still resent this levy and wonder what they personally gain from it.

In January 1959, the St. Andrews Golf Club offered Bobby Jones Honorary Membership of the club which he accepted in a very warm letter. The previous Autumn he had been made a freeman of St. Andrews. During his acceptance speech he used the often quoted sentence "I could take out of my life everything but my

Bobby Jones

ROBERT TYRE JONES, JR.
1425 C. & S. BANK BLDG.
ATLANTA, GEORGIA

January 13, 1959

G. E. Makin, Esq.
St. Andrews Golf Club
St. Andrews, Fife
Scotland

Dear Mr. Makin:

Thank you so much for your letter of January 9th.

Of course, I shall be very happy to be proposed for honorary membership in the St. Andrews Golf Club and honored to accept if elected.

You are kind to inquire of my health and the trip home. I must admit that parts of the journey, especially the flying, were a bit strenuous, but nothing could have prevented my availing myself of this opportunity to return to St. Andrews. The wonderful welcome accorded me there exceeded by far any hope that I might have had. The experience was one that I shall always cherish.

I enjoyed ever so much meeting you and the other officers and send you all my warmest regards and best wishes.

Most sincerely,

[signature]

RTJ:jsm

Letter from Bobby Jones

St. Andrews Golf Club Crest

122

experiences at St. Andrews and I'd still have a rich full life".

Above his picture which hangs in the clubhouse, is recorded his finest victories - three British Opens, four American Opens, one British Amateur Championship and five American Amateur Championships. 1930 saw his unforgettable and unrepeatable Grand Slam.

Some golf champions confine their moments of grace to compiling winning rounds. Not so Bobby Jones - he was the complete golfer and the complete gentleman.

At the end of 1959 we installed a Golf Ball machine which paid out the winners in golf balls. Its introduction was not trouble-free. Immediately a local golf shop protested about its possible loss of sales and soon after members found out how to cheat the machine and acquire free golf balls.

The Golf Ball machine was the forerunner of the gambling machines which we know. In 1962 we decided to install "an electrically operated, silent running 'fruit machine'". These machines revolutionised golf clubs' finances throughout Britain. In the last thirty years they have contributed a very large sum to our funds and kept subscriptions substantially lower than they would otherwise have been.

About this time our club crest was laid out at the entrance of the club at a cost of £96. I wonder how many times it has been photographed since then.

I enjoyed an entry scribbled on a copy of an A.G.M. agenda of the period. Obviously one member had been harassing the Captain and a helpful Secretary had scribbled a note "He does not have Meeting's support!! Just thank him for his comments and leave it." The soft answer turneth away wrath!

1968 saw the celebration of the Club's 125th birthday. The dinner was held in the Lumsden wing of the University.

The Wheatley recommendations for the reorganisation of Local Government were issued in 1970. The implications for golf in St. Andrews were considerable. The original proposal would have resulted in Fife being run from Dundee but this was fought off and instead Fife Region came into being. The abolition of the Town Council would have left the running of the courses in the hands of the District Council in Cupar.

To avoid this a new Links Trust Act 1974 was drawn up to maintain local control of the St. Andrews Courses. This was a hotch-potch based on the Acts of 1894, 1913, 1948 and 1953 and left local golfers on the outside looking in at a Trust and Management Committee in which they have little direct input. Not surprisingly this has led to friction which continues to the present day - and will continue. Our Club's Minutes record endless disputes with the Town Council and the R&A.

In 1969 Tony Jacklin won the Open at Royal Lytham & St. Annes. In 1970 he followed this by winning the U.S. Open by seven shots. In recognition of these outstanding achievements by a British golfer the Club invited him to become an

Bob Thomson receiving the 125th Anniversary Cup from the Captain

THE ST. ANDREWS GOLF CLUB
125th Anniversary Dinner
Star Hotel. St. Andrews
Monday 30th September 1968

After Dinner Sequence

1. Her Majesty the Queen.

2. "Our Guests" - Mr. A.C.Glencross, Captain

3. "Reply for the Guests" - Lt. Col. A.G.Brown

4. Presentation of Cups to 125th. Anniversary
    Competition Winners.

5. Song by Mr. Alistair Scott

6. "The St. Andrews Golf Club" -
    Provost T.T.Fordyce

7. "Reply for the St. Andrews Golf Club" -
    Mr. John L.Kinnear

8. Song by Mr. Alistair Scott

9. Presentation on behalf of Laurie Auchterlonie -
    Mr. F.J.Sturrock, Vice Captain

10. Song by Mr. Alistair Scott

11. Captain's closing remarks.

Left to Right
Mr. J.K. Wilson - Captain, Masonic G.C.
Mr. C.M. Todd - Chairman, Fife Golfing Assn.
Mr. John L. Kinnear, (partially hidden)
Mr. A.C. Glencross - CAPTAIN

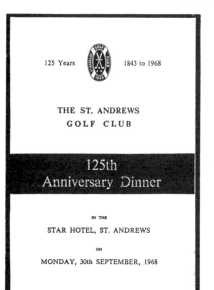

125 Years   1843 to 1968

THE ST. ANDREWS
GOLF CLUB

125th
Anniversary Dinner

IN THE

STAR HOTEL, ST. ANDREWS

ON

MONDAY, 30th SEPTEMBER, 1968

125 YEARS   ST. ANDREWS GOLF CLUB

125th ANNIVERSARY
CELEBRATION
DINNER

1843-1968

Monday, 30th September 1968
in the Star Hotel
St. Andrews

TICKETS 20/- 25/-   7.30 p.m. for 8 p.m.
DRESS OPTIONAL

125

Honorary Member. These four entries tell the rest of the story.

Monday 13th July 1970

"Mr. Jacklin intimated his acceptance with pride and pleasure but it was not possible to fix a date for a presentation ceremony at this time."

Monday 14th September 1970

"The Secretary reported that he had received no reply to his recent letter to Tony Jacklin and it was agreed that no further action, in the meantime, be taken."

Tuesday 20th October 1970

"A letter from Tony Jacklin was received. He said he would try to visit the Club in 1971."

Monday 11th February 1974

"Mr. Tony Jacklin has not yet visited the Club and the Presentation Box containing the plaque, scroll and Club tie are held in the safe and are now showing signs of decay."

Our next offer of Honorary Membership had a happier ending. Before the 1978 Open the Club had invited Jack Nicklaus to join us. He accepted. His first two rounds in the Open that year were hard fought ones and Nicklaus came off the 18th green a tired man after his second round of 72. Despite this he came straight into the Clubhouse for the presentation. At the front door he saw the notice "No Spikes" and promptly took off his golf shoes. His hosts suggested this was unnecessary but he insisted that club rules should be obeyed. Thereafter he asked to see the building and padded round in his socks. Jack Nicklaus made a lot of friends in the St. Andrews Club that day.

Within 48 hours he had scored two 69's to win the Open Championship, edging out Simon Owen in a last hole thriller. As a club member, his name went up on our Roll of Honour in the entrance hall along with the Club's other Open Championship winners.

One other Honorary Member joined the Club when Michael Bonallack was given this position in November 1990. His amateur record is unmatched - nine Walker Cup appearances, five Amateur Championships, four English Amateur Championships. In addition, through his work with the R&A, firstly on various committees and since 1983 as Secretary, Michael Bonallack has made a very substantial contribution to golf administration in Britain. The St. Andrews Club is honoured by having him as a member.

No history of the St. Andrews Golf Club would be complete without mentioning the Ayton family. The death of Laurie Ayton, Jnr. in 1989 marked the end of a direct five generation association with this club.

William Ayton, Snr., cabinet maker, is listed as one of our eleven founder

126

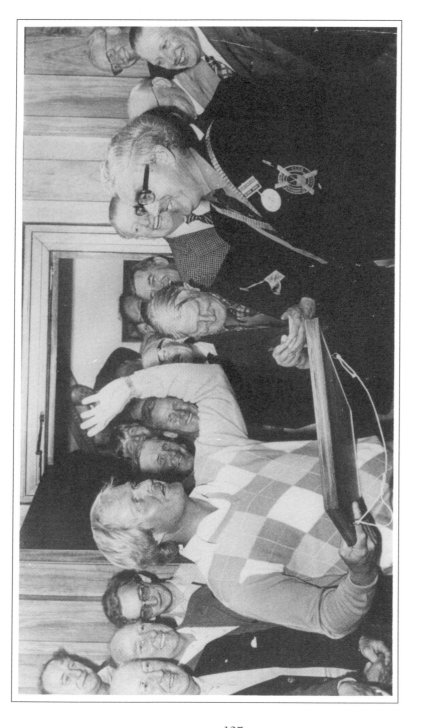

George Grant, captain, presenting Jack Nicklaus with his Honorary membership during the 1978 Open (The picture is used by kind permission of the Dundee Courier)

Michael Bonallack

members. Records suggest that he had fought at the battle of Trafalgar. He became our third Captain in 1846.

His son William Ayton, Jnr. was one of the key figures who held the Club together throughout the last century, when other town clubs were appearing and disappearing. In January 1895 the members presented him with a silver mounted walking stick to mark his fifty years with us, including 13 years as Captain - an outstanding contribution.

David, his son, does not appear in the club records as an administrator but he, like his grandfather and father, was a very talented golfer.

His four sons, Dave, Laurie, George and Alex all became first class golfers themselves. After serving in the First World War, they all went to professional posts in Canada and the U.S.A.

Eventually Dave and Laurie came back to the town and for years were very well known golfing personalities as players and as teachers. Laurie became Club Captain in 1953.

Laurie Ayton, Jnr. played in the professional circuit and was in the 1949 Ryder Cup team. He came back to the town in 1979, and took up his Club membership again. His funeral took place on 25th February 1989, the day his fellow members were playing for the Ayton trophy, presented to the club by Alex Ayton in 1946 - a strangely fitting end to the family's 147 years of club membership.

As a memorial the family have established a very generous fund to provide help to junior club members who show outstanding promise as golfers.

It is sad that Laurie did not live long enough to sit down with us at our Dinner celebrating the Club's one hundred and fifty years. He could have looked back on a club with a most impressive history, its records full of the names of the nineteenth century's golfing giants and one of which the first William Ayton would not have felt ashamed.

William Ayton, Captain (1846)

To conclude this History, I cannot improve on the words of James Sorley who rounded off his series of newspaper articles in 1911 thus:-

"The Records are finished and we have followed the

fortunes of the old Club from its humble start when a little band of enthusiasts first conceived the idea of forming a golf club, little dreaming that the evolution would be the now famous and powerful St. Andrews Golf Club."

"What we owe to them we cannot estimate. Certain are we all of this, that they sowed and we have reaped the fruits of their labours."

"Life is full of comparisons. We have a thousand blessings to thank our forefathers for and the pity is that the youth of today are too apt to forget this. If some of us would occasionally give a little time for quiet reflection

L.B. Ayton, Captain (1953)

and look around us casting our thoughts, for the moment, away back fifty or more years ago, I am afraid we would be bound to admit to ourselves that there is a deep debt of gratitude which we owe to those who have lived and laboured before us which can never be repaid in full."

"My task is completed. It remains now for me to add that I fervently hope and trust that the St. Andrews Golf Club will go on from prosperity to prosperity. May the members rally round the old Club and give these worthy men at the head of affairs that help which is so necessary to success and may concord and agreement be the happy spirit which animates all."

CLUB TROPHIES

1846 THE CAPTAIN'S TROPHY
This was first played for on New Year's Day 1847, our first medal Competition and is now the pendant on the Captain's chain of office.

1849 SPRING SCRATCH MEDAL
This is inscribed "St. Andrews Operatives Club". The club disbanded and their medal was passed on to the club.

1850 THE CROSS CLUBS
Originally this was second prize in the medal. Later it became The Spring Handicap Trophy.

1856 AUTUMN SCRATCH MEDAL
This was purchased for £3.9s. by members' subscription.

1889 AUTUMN HANDICAP MEDAL
This is for the best net return in the Autumn Meeting.

1894 THE JUBILEE CUP
Originally a stroke play competition, this is now one of the major knockout trophies. The story of its purchase is told elsewhere.

1902 THE HUGON CORONATION CUP
This commemorates the Coronation of King Edward VII and is, with the Jubilee Cup, one of our major match play trophies.

1903 DIAMOND JUBILEE MEDAL
The Medal was bought to mark the Club's 60th birthday. The first Class Winner of the Medal Finals receives this.

1906 McGREGOR TROPHY
This is played for by the winners of the alternative Thursday Medal competitions.

1910 THE GUY CAMPBELL CUP
One of the Club's major trophies, it is a Foursomes Match Play competition over the Old Course.

CLUB TROPHIES

Hugon Cup

Haig Cup

James Stewart
Coronation Cup

Boys' Championship
Cup

McGregor Trophy

Dr. Kyle Cup
Club Championship

John Macdonald
Seniors' Cup

Guy Campbell Cup

Jubilee Cup

Jock Hutchison
Cup

131

1910 THE AGGREGRATE MEDAL
Guy Campbell also presented this cup. It is given for the best aggregate scratch score in the Spring and Autumn Meetings.

1911 HAIG CUP
This is now awarded for one round of stroke play over optional courses.

1920 CHARLES GRIEVE CUP
This cup is awarded for one round of stroke play over the New Course.

1925 UNITED SERVICES CUP AND MEDAL
The United Services Association presented these trophies and they are awarded to the winner and runner-up for a one round stroke play competition.

1930 THE DR. KYLE MEMORIAL CUP
The Club Champion receives this trophy.

1935 JOCK HUTCHISON CUP
Jock Hutchison won the Open in 1921 and was a club member. There are two qualifying rounds. The best 32 then compete in match play for his trophy.

1937 SENIORS' CUP
Mr John Macdonald presented this cup for competition among senior members over 50 years of age.

1937 JAMES STEWART CUP
Mr. James Stewart while Vice Captain gave this trophy to commemorate the Coronation of King George VI. It is a one round, stroke play competition for members aged 55 and over.

1945 CENTENARY SALVER
The Daily Mail gave this cup to commemorate the Club's first 100 years. It is a single round stroke play event.

1946 AYTON TROPHY
Alex Ayton, an Honorary Vice President, gave this trophy. It is a single round stroke play event on optional courses.

1952 DUNCAN MILLER MEDAL
The best scratch score by a player under 21 in the Autumn Meeting wins this medal.

1958 JAMES ALEXANDER TROPHY
Mr Alexander was the Old Course Starter.   His widow presented the trophy.
Committee members and past Captains compete for it.

1959 WILLIAM LAMOND TROPHY
William Lamond was Captain in 1953-56.   This is a foursomes stroke play
competition played on the New Course.

1961 E.P. KYLE CUP
Mr. Kyle gave this when an Honorary Vice President.   Played on the Eden, it is a
foursome stroke play competition.

1966 JACK JOLLY TROPHY
This is given to the player with the best net aggregate over the Spring and Autumn
Meetings. Jack Jolly was an Honorary Vice President of the club.

1975 (1925) THE FIVE CLUB TROPHY
In 1925 the Club Captain Mr. James Spence provided a rustless iron shaft and Mr.
Wm. McLaren (Committee Member) provided a putter head. The Trophy was played
originally for as "The Visitors' Putter" by visitors in monthly competitions. The
competition stopped in 1939 at the start of the war. In 1975 a Five Club Competition
was introduced as an 18 hole stroke play over the Eden Course and the Visitors' Putter
was re-designed as the Competition Trophy.

1975 THE HAMADA TROPHY
Teams of three players compete for this cup.

1975 THE CAPTAIN'S TROPHY
In 1975, the Vice Captain, Mr. Tom Gordon, presented the trophy to the club. This
was originally on 18 hole stroke play competition played on vacant Saturdays during
the winter but later changed to a Sunday in February.

1976 THE WILLIAM HOGG NEW YEAR'S DAY TROPHY
In 1976 Mr. William Hogg presented a Trophy for annual competition. The Trophy
is awarded on New Year's Day for the best net score.

1984 THE MUSSELBURGH SALVER
In 1984 Mr. and Mrs. Ivor Highley presented a Salver to be named "The Musselburgh
Salver" for the winners of the Mixed Foursomes' Trophy.

1985 THE FAMOUS GROUSE TROPHY

In 1985 Matthew Gloag & Co, the makers of Famous Grouse whisky, set up a national Shotgun Foursomes Competition and awarded the trophy to the winners of the club Qualifying Round.

1986 THE DUNCAN McGREGOR OLD COURSE CUP

In 1986 the Reverend Duncan McGregor presented this Trophy to be awarded for the best net aggregate score returned in the Spring and Autumn Meeting by a player over 65 years of age.

1986 THE W.J.M. LAMOND TROPHY

In 1986 the family of the late William Lamond (past Treasurer and Club President) presented this trophy as the Club Championship (Silver Section) Trophy for players with handicap of 11-16 only.

1986 THE LAW TROPHY

In 1986 Mr. and Mrs. L. Law presented a trophy as the Club's Championship (Bronze Section) Trophy for players with handicaps of 17 and over.

1990 THE SASAKI S.S.K. TROPHY

In 1990 Mr. Kikuchi of the S.S.K. Corporation Japan Ltd. presented this trophy for an annual Fourball Matchplay Competition, the players to have one high and one low handicap player in each pair.

1990 THE ALEX FAIRLIE MEMORIAL TROPHY

In 1990 Mrs. A. Fairlie, widow of   Alex Fairlie, who died on the course whilst playing a Monthly Medal, presented the trophy to the club.   The competition is a Seniors' Stroke Play competition.

1991 THE JAMES TERRY MEMORIAL TROPHY

In 1991 Mr. William Terry, son of the late James Terry (Vice President) presented a trophy on behalf of the family, to be played for annually. It is open to members aged 50 and over.

1992 THE ALEX NORMAND ROSEBOWL

Alex Normand's family presented this Rosebowl to be awarded for the best net score in the Spring Meeting from those players 55 years of age and over.

CLUB MEMBERS 1992

ERNEST W ADAM
ANDREW G ADAMS
EDWIN ADAMS
GORDON S ADAMS
JOHN F ADAMS
IAN W ADAMSON
ANDREW AITKEN
DAVID S ALLAN
WILLIAM ALLAN
BRYAN C ANDERSON
DANIEL W ANDERSON
JAMES ANDERSON
KEITH S ANDERSON
MICHAEL ANDERSON
MORRIS ANDERSON
THOMAS ANDERSON
THOMAS ANDERSON
DEREK L ANNAL
CHRISTOPHER ARCHER
COLIN S ARMITT
GORDON ARMSTRONG
JAMES S ASKINGS
DAVID B AUCKLAND
GEORGE A AVELING
WILLIAM AYTON
HENRY W BAILLIE
ALEXANDER BAIN
JOHN J BAIRD
ALAN R BAKER
CRAIG R BAKER
JOHN BALLANTYNE
JOHN BALLANTYNE
COLIN R BALSILLIE
PETER J BANKS
WILLIAM J BARCLAY
HECTOR BARLOW
DAVID BATCHELOR
SCOTT BATHGATE
GRAEME D BAXTER
KEVIN W BAXTER
WILLIAM BAXTER
ALEXANDER BAYNE
DEREK A BAYNE
DOUGLAS W BAYNE
GRAHAM A BELL
STEVEN A BELL
ALEX J BENNETT
JOHN B BERRY

GEORGE C BETTY
KEITH BEVAN
JOHN BIRRELL
ALEXANDER A BLACK
EWAN J BLACK
NORMAN BLACK
PETER S BLACK
THOMAS BLACK
ROBERT L BLACKWOOD
JOHN BLYTH
IAIN I BLYTHE
DEREK BOTTOMER
JAMES L BOWIE
RANALD G BOYD
JOHN BOYNE
JOHN T BRADLEY
CHARLES BRAID
DEREK BRANNAN
WALTER R D BRETT
ALAN BROADBENT
JOHN BROCKLEBANK
MICHAEL R BRODIE
RONALD W BRODIE
JOHN A BROMPTON
COLIN A BROWN
DAVID D BROWN
DAVID R BROWN
DAVID W BROWN
DAVID A H BROWN
JAMES G BROWN
JOHN BROWN
MARK J BROWN
NORMAN M BROWN
ROBERT W BROWN
ROBERT J BROWN
WILLIAM M BROWN
DAVID BROWN JNR
JAMES K BROWNLEE
COLIN M BRUCE
JAMES M BRUCE
PATRICK J BRUCE
RICHARD M BRUCE
WILLIAM BRUCE
ALBERT E BUCHANAN
JOHN Y BUDDO
JOHN A BUIST
BRIAN BURGESS
CLIVE D BURHOUSE

DOUGLAS A BURNETT
DAVID W BURNS
JOHN CAIRNS
ALAN C CAITHNESS
COLIN H CAMERON
DUNCAN M CAMERON
EUAN G CAMERON
ROBERT G CAMERON
ALAN H CAMPBELL
DONALD CAMPBELL
ROBERT G CAMPBELL
THOMAS CAMPBELL
ALEXANDER D CANNON
WILLIAM S CANTLAY
WILLIAM R CARGILL
WILLIAM CARGILL
ALAN CARLYLE
IAN CARRADICE
JAMES P CARRUTHERS
ROBERT B CARSON
ANDREW CARSTAIRS
ANDREW CARSTAIRS JNR
JAMIE CARVER
NORMAN L CATHRO
FRANCIS S CHAPLIN
GEORGE CHRISTIE
GORDON CHRISTIE
IAN CHRISTIE
MICHAEL CHRISTIE
ROBERT C CHRISTIE
STUART CHRISTIE
MICHAEL J CIESLA
BRIAN CLARK
DAVID B CLARK
DOUGLAS CLARK
ERIC D CLARK
HAMISH S M CLARK
JACK CLARK
JAMES S CLARK
JAMES CLARK
JOHN D CLARK
WILLIAM D CLARK
MATTHEW W CLOSE
GAVIN B COBB
GRAEME M COBB
RAYMOND S COCHRANE
JAMES K COCKBURN
BRIAN C COLLIN

IAN G COLLINS
ANDREW CONNAL
ARTHUR CONNELLY
GEORGE W CONNELLY
IAN G CONNELLY
MICHAEL H CONNELLY
BRIAN W COOK
EDWARD COOK
R MORTON COOPER
WILLIAM A COOPER
WILLIAM J CORMACK
JAMES CORSTORPHINE
STUART CORSTORPHINE
FRANCIS E COUGAN
FINLAY J COULL
ETHELBERT COWE
JOHN COYLE
GEORGE CRAIG
KENNETH CRAIG
STEWART CRAM
GORDON CRAMB
RONALD C CRAMB
GRAHAM A CRICHTON
JOHN B CRICHTON
WILLIAM CRICHTON
WILLIAM G CRICHTON
FRED H CRISP
JAMES K CROWE
ROBERT J CROWE
GEORGE CUBBAGE
ALAN J CUMMING
BARRY G CUNDY
ALEXANDER CUNNINGHAM
ALEXANDER H CUNNINGHAM
ANDREW CUNNINGHAM
BRIAN CUNNINGHAM
DENNIS CUNNINGHAM
GEORGE M CUNNINGHAM
IAN CUNNINGHAM
JAMES G CUNNINGHAM
JAMES A CUNNINGHAM
GEORGE K CURRIE
JAMES H CURRIE
ALEXANDER M CUTHBERT
THOMAS DARROCH
COLIN DAVIDSON
HENRY J DAVIDSON
RICHARD H DAVIDSON

135

WILLIAM DAVIDSON
GEORGE M DAVIDSON JNR
GORDON S DAVIE
ROBERT G DEACON
ROBERT F DEANE
ROBERT DEAS
WILLIAM DEAS
IAN S DEMPSTER
RICHARD S DERRICK
THOMAS DEVANEY
JOHN DEVLIN
ANDREW K DEWAR
IAN T DICKSON
ANDREW DINGWALL
J G DISHINGTON
GRAHAM E DIXON
PETER DIXON
JOHN DOBBIN
JOHN DOBSON
NEIL C DOBSON
NORMAN W DOBSON
ANDREW DONALDSON
DAVID DONALDSON
GEORGE DONALDSON
IAIN M DONALDSON
JOHN DONALDSON
MALCOLM DONALDSON
PETER J DONALDSON
ROBERT C DONALDSON
STANLEY C DONALDSON
STEPHEN W DONALDSON
THOMAS DONALDSON
GERALD W DONLON
IAN M DONLON
JOHN M DONNACHIE
SANDY DOUGLAS
THOMAS R DOUGLAS
ERNEST G DOW
JAMES M DOW
W I DOW
FRASER DOWIE
THOMAS DOWIE
JAMES DOYLE
JAMES C DRUMMOND
ANDREW D DRYSDALE
MALCOLM L DRYSDALE
ROY DUFF
GRAHAM K DUNCAN
MALCOLM DUNCAN
ALEXANDER D DUNN
JOHN DUNN

WILLIAM L DUNNE
PATRICK EARLEY
PATRICK J EARLEY
ALEX H EDDIE
ROBERT A EDIE
WILLIAM EDIE
SCOTT EDWARDS
STEVE EGGO
MARK C EGLINTON
A STEWART ELDRIDGE
ALAN D ELLIOTT
GRAHAM G EMMERSON
CHRISTOPHER EMMOTT
J A EMSLIE
JAMES ERSKINE
CHARLES R ESCHENFELDER
ROBERT M ESPIE
THOMAS C B EWAN
ROBERT C EYNON
JAMES FAIRBAIRN
JAMES FALLS
PETER M FALLS
JAMES C FARMER
DONALD FEARNLEY
DENNIS FEGAN
JOHN C FENTON
LENNOX C FENTON
RONALD FENTON
CHARLES A FERGUSON
JAMES F FERGUSON
ROBERT FERGUSON
ROBERT C FERGUSON
STEVEN G FERGUSON
ALISTAIR FERRIER
DAVID FERRIER
WILLIAM B FERRIER
DAVID FERRIER JNR
ALAN FINLAY
CHARLES A FINLAY
COLIN C FINLAY
DAVID FINLAY
NICOLL FINLAY
STEPHEN P FINLAY
ADAM FINNIE
GORDON G FISHER
JOHN G FISHER
JACK C FLEMING
JAMES FLEMING
JAMES FLYNN
JAMES FLYNN JNR
IAN A FORBES

THOMAS FORD
DOUGLAS F FORSTER
CAMPBELL FRASER
ALEXANDER FREEDMAN
ROBERT H GADD
THOMAS GALLACHER
ALAN GARDINER
IAN R GARDNER
WILLIAM S GARDNER
KENNETH GARLAND
JOHN GATHERUM
JOHN A GATHERUM
RAYMOND M GATHERUM
STUART GATHERUM
TIMOTHY C GATHERUM
SCOTT GEORGE
DAVID M GIBSON
ERIC GILLESPIE
EDWARD GILMOUR
STUART GIVEN
CHRISTOPHER R GLENDINNING
DEREK G GORDON
GEORGE GORDON
GEORGE A GORDON
JAMES A GORDON
PHILIP GORDON
STUART GORDON
THOMAS GORDON
BRUCE S GOUDIE
ALEXANDER H GOURLAY
DAVID A GOURLAY
DOUGLAS F GOURLAY
JOHN G GOURLAY
JOHN H GOURLAY
PETER GOVAN
EDWARD S GRAHAM
JOHN M GRAHAM
WILLIAM J GRAHAM
GARRY A GRANT
GEORGE GRANT
IAN L GRANT
JOHN M GRANT
THOMAS GRANT
JAMES GRAY
JOHN D GRAY
STEWART GRAY
WILLIAM GREEN
ANDREW GREENWOOD
KENNETH GREENWOOD
SAMUEL GREENWOOD
SEAN GREENWOOD

DAVID GREIG
JOHN F GREIG
J P GRIBBEN
JAMES S GRIERSON
ANDREW GRIEVE
ANGUS GRIEVE
GEOFFREY W GRIFFITHS
ROGER L GUEST
GRIEVE F GUTHRIE
MARTIN F GUTHRIE
HARRY B GUYAN
KEITH HAIG
ALAN D HAMILTON
ANDREW N HAMILTON
DAVID W HAMILTON
ROY A HAMILTON
THOMAS C HAMILTON
JAMES B HARLEY
RICHARD A HARRIS
GEORGE HART
SCOTT HART
RAYMOND M HASSALL
JAMES HASTIE
KEVIN HASTIE
MARTIN J HASTIE
HENRY S HASTON
COLIN D HAY
NEIL HAYLES
RICHARD K HEFFERNAN
ALISTAIR A HEGGIE
DONALD C HEGGIE
JAMES HENDERSON
JOHN J HENDERSON
NORMAN C HENDERSON
T G HENDERSON
ROBERT H HENRIT
SAMUEL G HENRY
ANDREW HERD
DAVID HERD
DAVID HERD
MICHAEL J HERD
RONALD M HERD
STEVEN R HERD
GARY HOOD
MICHAEL J HOPKINS
DOUGLAS HOPTON
MARK A HORN
NICHOLAS D HORN
SAMUEL A HORN
SYDNEY J HORN
BRIAN HOUSTON

IAN M HOWE
JAMES J HOWE
GEORGE HUGHES
JACK H HUMPHRIES
JOHN HUMPHRIES
MICHAEL J HUMPHRIES
IAIN HUNTER
JAMES C HUNTER
JAMES HUNTER
ROBERT HYNDMAN
CLIVE R IRVINE
GAVIN R IRVINE
JOHN A IRVINE
GREGOR JACK
RONALD W JACKSON
ELLIS G JAFFRAY
JAMES T JAMIESON
LAURENCE A JAMISON
ALFRED L JANNETTA
LYN J JENKINS
JAMES M JENKINSON
CHARLES JOBSON
WILLIAM A JOHNSON
ALASTAIR JOHNSTON
ANDREW JOHNSTON
DAVID A JOHNSTON
KENNETH A JOHNSTON
ROY D JOHNSTON
STUART J K JOHNSTONE
ANDREW S JONES
DAVID JOY
IAN JOY
TREVOR KAY
JOHN KEENAN
JOHN C KEIR
KENNETH W KEIR
JOHN KELLY
ALAN J KEMP
GRAHAM D KEMP
STEWART KEMP
JOHN F KEOGH
ANDREW T KERACHER
JAMES T KERACHER
MARK KERACHER
THOMAS M KERACHER
ARCHIBALD KERR
BARRY KERR
MICHAEL KIERNAN
MICHAEL J KINLOCH
NORMAN J KINLOCH
PATRICK I KINSLEY

GORDON KIRK
JOHN C KIRK
ROBERT S KIRK
DAVID E KIRKCALDY
PAUL KIRKCALDY
ROBERT KIRKCALDY
PETER KIRKLAND
DONALD W KNAGGS
JAMES M KNOX
RAJ KUMAR
JAMES LAHEY
STEWART H LAIDLAW
RONNIE LAING
ALEXANDER LAIRD
ROBERT LAMBERT
WILLIAM LAMOND
KENNETH LAMONT
GORDON C LANGLANDS
RONALD LANGLANDS
ALEXANDER LATTO
BARRY J LATTO
DAVID T LATTO
PETER J LINNEY
GARRY LAU
WILLIAM F LAVER
COLIN W LAW
IAN C LAW
KEVIN LAW
WILLIAM LAW
EDWARD LAWLOR
DAVID LAWRIE
DUNCAN M LAWRIE
PHILIP LAWRIE
COLIN LAWSON
DAVID J LEE
RICHARD G LEES
DAVID M LEITH
WILLIAM C LENNIE
ERIC R LIDDELL
BARRIE D LIDDLE
HENRY H LIDDLE
KENNETH L LINDSAY
DALE G LISTER
ERIC LITTON
DAVID A LIVINGSTONE
THOMAS LIVINGSTONE
ALEXANDER LORIMER
ARTHUR C LORIMER
DAVID M LOW
JAMES W LOW
ANDREW LUMSDEN

ANDREW K LUMSDEN
IAIN M LUMSDEN
J R LUMSDEN
JAMES H LUMSDEN
ROBERT S LUMSDEN
DAVID LYALL
DAVID J LYALL
HARRY M LYNCH
GEORGE MacCONNOCHIE
IAN MACDONALD
JAMES N MACDONALD
JAMES MacFARLANE
JAMES W MACGREGOR
R MACIVER
GEORGE MACKAY
WALTER L MACKAY
FINLAY MACKENZIE
ROBERT MACKENZIE
GERALD MACKIE
JAMES MACKIE
JAMES B MACKIE
JOHN B MACKIE
THOMAS S MACKIE
GAVIN N MACLEOD
JOHN F MACLEOD
JOHN S MACPHERSON
HECTOR W MAIN
WILLIAM MAIN
JOHN A MAKEIN
DAVID MALCOLM
EDWARD MALCOLM
THOMAS G MALCOLM
HAMISH MARSHALL
JOHN R MARSHALL
PAUL MARSHALL
SAMUEL M MARSHALL
ARCHIBALD N MARTIN
CHARLES K MATHER
HARRY D MATHESON
ALAN MATHEWSON
ERIC MATHEWSON
NEIL MATHEWSON
WILLIAM MATHEWSON
DENNIS A MATTHEWS
IAIN M MATTHEWS
EBENEZER MAUCHLINE
ALEXANDER N MAULE BEN
ALEXANDER M MAXWELL
GRAHAM K McALLISTER
BRUCE A MCEWAN
GORDON McGLADE

JOHN M McMILLAN
HAMISH McNICOLL
COLIN McSHANE
JAMES S McARTHUR
WILLIAM McATEER
JOHN J McBREARTY
DONALD McBRIDE
ROBERT McCABE
JAMES McCAIRNS
DUNCAN McCALLUM
JAMES R McCARTNEY
ARCHIBALD C McCLURE
ROBERT McCLYMONT
THOMAS McCOLL
NORMAN McCONNACHIE
STEPHEN McCONNELL
JOHN McCONVILLE
CHARLES McDONALD
GILBERT McDONALD
WILLIAM J McDONALD
JOHN McEWAN
STEPHEN McFARLANE
CHARLES McGINLEY
PATRICK McGINLEY
ANDREW S McGLASHAN
JOHN D McGOWAN
PAUL J McGRATH
DAVID McGREGOR
ALISTAIR McHARDY
EWAN G McINTOSH
KEITH McINTOSH
ROBERT McINTOSH
WILLIAM F McINTOSH
ALEXANDER D McKECHNIE
JAMES S McKECHNIE
MARTIN D McKECHNIE
JOHN McKIE
ALISTAIR S McLEAN
ANGUS F McLEAN
NEIL McLEAN
PETER McLEAN
STEWART I McLEAN
GORDON McLEOD
RANDAL McLISTER
JOHN McNABB
JOHN McNABB
RODERICK McNEIL
BRIAN D McQUEEN
GRAEME E McQUEEN
ANDY McROBBIE
ARCHIBALD McROBBIE

137

ROBERT B MEECHIE
JAMES K MEEK
WILLIAM S A MELDRUM
ALEXANDER L MELVILLE
DAVID G MELVILLE
JAMES MELVILLE
JOHN MELVILLE
DAVID G MELVILLE JNR
JAMES MENZIES
JAMES M MENZIES
PETER H MENZIES
JOHN S METHVEN
STEVEN J METHVEN
WILLIAM METHVEN
ALAN W MILLAR
ROBERT S MILLAR
ROBERT D MILLAR
DAVID W MILLER
DAVID J MILLER
DAVID J MILLER
DOUGLAS W D MILLER
ALEC MILNE
DOUGLAS W MILNE
ERNEST MILNE
JAMES E MILNE
BRIAN J MINTO
ROGER J MINTO
ANGUS M MITCHELL
COLIN MITCHELL
DAVID H MITCHELL
G MURRAY MITCHELL
JAMES M MITCHELL
JOHN MITCHELL
BRIAN MOFFAT
DAVID MOFFAT
JOHN A MOFFAT
ROBERT W MOFFAT
GORDON A MOIR
ROBERT G MONCUR
GORDON A MONTGOMERY
ERIC MORAN
MAGNUS MORE
ALAN MORGAN
CHARLES S MORGAN
A A MORRIS
RALPH H MORRIS
PETER MORRISON
RONALD MORRISON
IAN MORTON
JOSEPH I MORTON
THOMAS MORTON

CAMPBELL J B MURDOCH
PETER F MURNIN
ANDREW MURRAY
GEORGE K MURRAY
ROBERT S MURRAY
THOMAS MUSTARD
HERBERT NANSON
KEITH A NANSON
G D NAPIER
ROBERT NAPTHINE
JOHN NEAL
HENRY A NELSON
BRIAN F NICHOLSON
DAVID NICHOLSON
GARY NICHOLSON
JOHN NICHOLSON
WILLIAM B NICOL
WILLIAM J NICOL
GARY J NICOLL
JOHN M NICOLL
JOHN M NICOLL
JOHN NICOLL
KEVIN W NICOLL
SCOTT NICOLL
WILLIAM J NICOLL
A CLARK NIVEN
ALBERT NIVEN
CLARK NIVEN
DUNCAN NIVEN
J GRAHAME NIVEN
STUART NIVEN
STUART M NIVEN
WALTER D NIVEN
DAVID NIVEN M.B.E., J.P.
JOSEPH C NOBLE
STUART F NORMAND
NICHOLAS O'BRIEN
WILLIAM J O'BRIEN
DEREK O'NEILL
SCOTT OGILVIE
WILLIAM J OGILVIE
NEIL P OGSTON
STEPHEN W OGSTON
GEORGE ORR
EMIL PACHOLEK
JOSEPH PALOMPO
MICHAEL J PARKS
TEOFIL PASEK
D STEVEN PATERSON
JOHN PATERSON
ALEXANDER PATON

NEIL PATON
JOHN PAYNE
BRIAN J PEATTIE
EDWARD PEATTIE
RONALD PENNYCOOK
ROGER PHILLIPS
JAMES PHILP
JOHN PHILP
IAN PIGGOT
HERBERT A PIRIE
MARTIN P PLAYFORD
ALAN POLLOCK
PETER POLSON
JOHN O B POOLMAN
KEVIN I PORTER
KENNETH W POTTS
ALEXANDER PRICE
GERALD PRIEST
DAVID PROCTOR
ALAN T PURDIE
DAVID J RABBITT
STEVEN RACE
GEORGE S RADLEY
ALISTAIR J RAE
IAN B RAMAGE
JOSEPH A RAMSAY
PETER RAMSAY
ROBERT RAMSAY
DAVID F RAYNOR
DAVID S RAYNOR
DAVID REDDIE
ALBERT S REED
LAURENCE W REED
ALEXANDER REEKIE
ROBERT REEKIE
ANGUS F REID
MARTIN REID
BRIAN REILLY
FRANK REILLY
THOMAS REILLY
ANDREW R RENDLE
STEPHEN A RICHARDSON
HAROLD L RIGG
DAVID G RINTOUL
ROY A RINTOUL
JOHN RITCHIE
NEIL ROBB
DAVID S ROBERTSON
IAN M ROBERTSON
JAMES G ROBERTSON
JOHN D B ROBERTSON

KENNETH B ROBERTSON
ROBERT S ROBERTSON
THOMAS ROBERTSON
THOMAS W ROBERTSON
THOMAS W ROBERTSON
TERENCE G ROBIE
JOHN S ROBINSON
CHARLES P RODGER
IAN RODGER
NEIL C RONALDSON
ALEXANDER J ROSE
IAIN ROSS
LAWRENCE M ROSS
RODERICK C ROSS
WILLIAM D ROSS
EDWARD ROTHERY
KENNETH ROUGH
ALEXANDER C ROWE
NEIL W ROWLEY
ALAN M RUSSELL
JAMES RUSSELL
THOMAS S RUSSELL
A B RUTHERFORD
JOHN D RYAN C.B.E.
CLIFFORD A SAFFRON
GRANT N SAMPSON
IAN H SCAMBLER
TERENCE SCANLON
ALEXANDER D SCOTT
ALEXANDER N SCOTT
ALEXANDER SCOTT
DAVID W SCOTT
GEORGE W SCOTT
HERBERT SCOTT
HUGH P SCOTT
JOHN SCOTT
MORRIS A SCOTT
RICHARD J SCOTT
DAVID SEELEY
MARSHALL T SHAND
JAMES SHANKS
GEORGE SHARP
KENNETH SHARP
ANDREW SHEPHERD
COLIN B SHEPHERD
DAVID C SHEPHERD
D BRIAN SHIELDS
RAYMOND SHORT
NEIL A SHOWELL
JAMES SIDEY
JAMES SIEVEWRIGHT

138

JAMES SIEVEWRIGHT JNR
JOHN W SIM
DAVID F SIMPSON
DAVID SIMPSON
G C M SIMPSON
IAN D SIMPSON
JOHN J SIMPSON
LENAIS SIMPSON
PHILIP W SINCLAIR
STEVEN SLADE
FRANK SLATER
HARRY J SMALL
DAVID B SMART
DOUGLAS B SMART
G DOUGLAS SMART
HENRY SMART
JAMES B SMART
ANDREW SMITH
DAVID J SMITH
JAMES SMITH
JAMES C SMITH
JAMES P SMITH
NORMAN M SMITH
PAT SMITH
WILLIAM L SMITH
JAMES SOMMERVILLE
JOHN SPEED
THOMAS SPEED
COLIN D SPEIGHT
DANIEL A SPEIGHT
JAMES B SPITTAL
ANDREW J STEPHEN
DOUGLAS STEPHEN
FORBES L STEPHEN
HAMISH F STEPHEN
RAYMOND STEPHENSON
SYDNEY J STEVENSON
SIDNEY STEVENSON SEN
DUNCAN STEWART
HARVEY R STEWART
JAMES K STEWART
MALCOLM STEWART
MARTIN STEWART
ROBERT STEWART
ROBERT STEWART
ROBERT D STEWART
RODERICK STEWART
JAMES K STEWART JNR
DAVID R STRACHAN
IAN I STRACHAN
RODDY K STURROCK

SIDNEY M SUMMERS
DONALD J SUTHERLAND
JOHN A SUTHERLAND
T A SUTHERLAND
ANDREW J SUTTIE
DAVID SWANKIE
IAN S SWANKIE
NICHOLAS A SWEENEY
BRIAN TAIT
CHRISTOPHER J TALBOT
MALCOLM D TALBOT
JOSEPH TARNOWSKI
MALCOLM G TAYLOR
THOMAS J TAYLOR
WILLIAM TERRY
ALEXANDER Mc G THOM
ANDREW C THOM
ARTHUR A THOM
KENNETH A THOM
MICHAEL J THOM
RONALD W THOM
ARTHUR THOM SNR
DAVID M THOMAS
STEPHEN G THOMPSON
BRIAN R THOMSON
DAVID C THOMSON
DENYS L THOMSON
GEORGE THOMSON
LEWIS THOMSON
PETER THOMSON
ROBERT THOMSON
FREDERICK A TIDMARSH
TERRY P TILBERRY
ALEXANDER H TODD
ALEXANDER H TODD
CHARLES M TODD
NEIL A TODD
ANDREW TOMLINSON
ANDY TOPPING
JOHN TORRIE
DUNCAN TOSH
ALAN C TULLETH
ALASTAIR B TULLETH
WILLIAM TULLETH JNR
A ROGER TULLOCH
ROY VERNER
GERALD H VOSE
C GEORGE O WALKER
GRAHAM WALKER
RONALD D K WALKER
DAVID M WALLACE

JAMES B WALLACE
ROSS F WALLACE
CLIVE WALLIS
ANDREW M WARREN
JOHN S WARRENDER
WILLIAM B WATERS
DAVID WATSON
IAN W WATSON
JAMES A WATSON
ROSS WATSON
WILLIAM R WATSON
MICHAEL WEAVER
GRAEME J WEBSTER
TOM WEBSTER
ALEXANDER WEIR
IAN WEIR
IAN A WELCH
JACK M WELCH
NEIL G WESTWOOD
D GRANT L WHITE
GARY WHITE
JOHN R WHITE
DAVID WHITELAW
IAN A WHITELAW
THOMAS Y WHITTET
DAVID WILKIE
HARRY F WILKIE
WILLIAM WILKINSON
JAMES A WILLIAMSON
ALEXANDER N WILSON
CHARLES A WILSON
DOUGLAS R WILSON
GERALD WILSON
HARRY K WILSON
IAN W WILSON
JAMES G WILSON
JOHN S WILSON
JONATHAN J WILSON
LEWIS WILSON
ROBERT WILSON
THOMAS WILSON
IAN WINN
SINCLAIR WINSKILL
SCOTT C WINSLOW
A S WONG
ALAN WONG
RICHARD M WOOD
JAMES WOODS
WALTER WOODS B.E.M.
ANDREW C WRIGHT
KENNETH C WRIGHT

CRAIG W WYLIE
DAVID YOUNG
IAN L YOUNG
STEVEN A ZAMORA

139

COUNTRY MEMBERS 1992

ALBERT W ADAM
DAVID A AINSWORTH
JAMES P ALEXANDER
ALEXANDER ALLAN
ROBERT ALLAN
ALEX ALLARDICE
JOHN ALLARDICE
BRIAN ANDERSON
EWAN J ANDERSON
GORDON C ANDERSON
JOHN ANNAND
WILLIAM ARCHIBALD
ADAM I ARMSTRONG
IAN B BAKER
GLEN BALLANTYNE
GRAHAM G BARCLAY
DEREK BAYLEY
YUILLE BAYLEY
GEORGE BISSET
JEFFREY T BOND
TERENCE W BOND
MICHAEL J BONNER
DAVID J BONTHRON
W KENNETH BOWIE
ARCHIBALD N BROWN
PETER A BROWN
THOMSON J BROWN
RICHARD J BROWNING
JOHNATHAN M BRUNSON
DAVID A BUIST
JAMES BULLOCH
A CAMPBELL BURN
BRIAN J BUTCHER
DUNCAN CALDER
THOMAS M CALLENDER
JOHN A CAMPBELL
LACHLAN M CARVER
KEITH CHALMERS
ARTHUR CHECKLEY
ANDREW CHRISTIE
TERENCE J CLARK
JOHN L CLINK
JOHN A COAD
JAMES N COCHRAN
JOHN P COLES
GERARD COLGAN
MICHAEL N COLLINS
MICHAEL J COLLINS

JOHN A COLLINSON
PETER CONN
DAVID W CRICHTON
DOUGLAS R CRICHTON
JOHN CORMACK
DUNCAN CURRIE
GEORGE W CURRIE
RONALD DAVIES
SIMON J DAVIES
WILLIAM DAVIES
CHARLES DAWSON
HERBIE DAYAL
ALAN G DEVLIN
ANDREW F DEWAR
GARY DICKSON
JOHN D DICKSON
TIMOTHY C DINAN
PHILIP A DORAN
PETER A DRYSDALE
MICHAEL DUDDY
IAN DUNCAN
WILLIAM DUNN
THOMAS A DYER
IAN R EDMISTON
IAN M EMSLIE
GRAHAM E EVERETT
CHRISTOPHER P EYNON
IAN FALCONER
DAVID S FINLAY
A D FISHER
IAN J FLEMING
JONATHAN R FORSYTH
ARTHUR J FOSTER
STEPHEN J FOSTER
ROBERT C FOTHERINGHAM
WILLIAM FOULTON
WILTON J FRANCIS
STUART E FRASER
JAMES FRIEL
PAUL FRIEL
DAVID B GALLETLY
JAMES W GILCHRIST
ANDREW G GRANT
WILLIAM G GRANT
DON HAINES
ALAN S HAIRE
NIGEL S HAMMILL
JOHN A HARVEY

C BRYAN HASTON
MALCOLM HATCH
COLIN J HAWORTH
JACK HAWORTH
PATRICK J HAYCOCK
JOHN N HEFFERNAN
JOHN J HENDERSON
BRIAN HENDRY
BRUCE HENDY-POOLEY
IAIN J HIGHLEY
IVOR A HIGHLEY SNR
IVOR A HIGHLEY JNR
IAN D HODGE
WILLIAM S HODGSON
DEREK F R HORN
STEPHEN W HORN
CHRISTOPHER HOSKING
NORMAN E HOWE
RONALD R HUSH
DAVID M HUTCHISON
NORMAN B HUTTON
A GRAEME HYSLOP
PAUL A INCERTI
DENYS INGHAM
YOSHIMASA IROBE
JAMES JARVIE
CHARLES I JOBSON
JAMES T JOHNSTON
TIMOTHY S JONES
SAMAD KADER
SHOICHI KAYABA
JOHN G KELLY
PETER A KERACHER
JAMES KERR
ROBERT KERR
MAX KIMOTO
DAVID KIRK
DUNCAN KIRK
YUZURU KOGA
RICHARD J LAING
MICHAEL G LAMB
JAMES A R M LESSELS
ALEXANDER LETHAM
LAWRENCE N LEVY
WILLIAM G LIDDELL
LAURENCE J LIDDLE
JAMES S LINDSAY
ADRIAN LINNEY

DAVID A LIVINGSTONE
JEREMY J LOCKER
ANDREW D N LOWE
WILLIAM M LYLE
NEILE MACARTHUR
IAN R MACFADYEN
ROBERT P MACKAY
COLIN J MACKIE
JOHN L MACKIE
MALCOLM D MACKINNON
NORMAN K MacKINNON
MALCOLM S MacLEOD
IAIN G MACPHERSON
THOMAS N MALCOLM
ROBERT A MANSON
CLIVE G HARRISON
ARCHIBALD MARSHALL
DENIS H MARTIN
RONALD W MATHEWSON
ROBERT C MATTHEWS
GREG MAUCHLINE
DANIEL McGUINNESS
COLIN D McARTHUR
ANGUS McCALLUM
MILES V McCANN
ALEXANDER P McDONALD
WILLIAM McDONALD
PETER McGAHAN
COLIN J McGEOCH
DUNCAN J McGREGOR
DOUGLAS McGUFFIE
ROBERT O McINNES
JAMES A McINTOSH
IAN D McLAREN
WILLIAM A McLEAN
THOMAS E MELVILLE
COLIN MENZIES
WILLIAM C METHVEN
DAVID D MILLAR
STEWART MILNE
DOUGLAS J MITCHELL
SCOTT A MITCHELL
BRIAN D MORGAN
DENNIS F MORGAN
KENNETH J MORRIS
ALAN MORRISON
JOHN MOSES
GEORGE F MOYES

PATRICK J MULQUEEN

PAUL G MULVEY

NORIYUKI MURAKAMI

ALAN MURRAY

CHARLES R J MURRAY

JOHN K NAPIER

TOM NEGORO

GEORGE R NELSON

STEPHEN NELSON

ALEXANDER W NICOL

HAROLD OGDEN

NEIL OGSTON

RON PATERSON

ANDREW G PATRICK

ROBERT J PEDRETT

JAMES PENNYCOOK

THOMAS PHILBIN

MARTIN C POPE

CHARLES P POSNETT

ALASTAIR V POWRIE

ROBERT PRYDE

GEORGE A RADLEY

MICHAEL RAJ

MALCOLM A RAMSAY

ALAN J RAND

TOM RANKIN

IAN P REDFORD

JOHN R REEKIE

A RONALD S REID

ATHOLE M REID

FRANCIS S RENNIE

STUART E REPTON

GEORGE M C RIDDICK

BRIAN RIGG

JAMES W RITCHIE

GORDON ROBERTS

NORMAN J ROBERTSON

WILLIAM J ROBERTSON

LEWIS M RODGER JNR

COLIN RONALD

DAVID P ROSE

MICHAEL C ROSKELL

IAN RUSSELL

DOUGLAS M SCOTT

TERENCE SCOTT

WILLIAM SCOTT

WILLIAM R SCOTT

JACK SCRIMSHIRE

MARK P SEDWILL

GRAEME SEELEY

HUGH SMITH

WILLIAM B SMITH

WILLIAM SMITH

LAWRENCE A SNYDER

PHILIP SOMERS

DAVID M SPENS

BRIAN D STEEL

ARCHIBALD STEWART

LESLIE M STEWART

PAUL STEWART

SYDNEY STRIDE

RICHARD J STURROCK

ALAN J TERZZA

RHYS E THOMAS

JAMES A THOMPSON

STEPHEN THORNBER

SHINICHIRO TORII

ARMENIO TREVISAN

PAUL TREVISAN

OSAMU TSUKASA

PETER S USHER

GEORGE S VEITCH

ANTHONY VETTRAINO

MATTHEW WADDELL

IAIN WALLACE

PATRICK WARD

STUART S WATERS

THOMAS WATSON

DARREN C WEBB

DOUGLAS E WEBSTER

JOHN WEST

BRUCE D WHEELAN

GAVIN WHYTE

ALAN WILKINSON

JACK M WILLOUGHBY

ALEXANDER W C WILSON

JAMES WILSON

LEON D WILTSHIRE

KENNETH U WRIGHT

GORDON J WYLIE

PATRICK J YADE

CHRISTOPHER J ZOCHOWSKI

OVERSEAS MEMBERS 1992

JALAL AHMED

MASAKUNI AKIYAMA

ROBERT L ALBRITTON

BILL C ALDORSSON

BEN AMATO

HAMISH ANDERSON

PHILIP R ANDERSON

WILLIAM G ANDERSON

GABOR S ANTALICS

TAKESHI AOKI

RICO ARNOSTI

ALEXANDER AUER

PHILIP S BARRETT

KARL ERNST BERGER

WAYNE B BIBLE

ALEXANDER BLACK

DAVID BOOTH

ROMEO J BORELLA

JOSEPH BOWMAN

HUGH P BOWMAN

WILLIAM S BOWMAN

STEPHEN BOYD

IAN M BROWN

HANS BRUNHOEBER

JOHANNES F BUURMAN

STERLING CALL

RAYMOND R CALLAWAY

WILLIAM CAMPBELL

ANDREW A CARIDIS

JOSEPH P CARNEY

ALBERT E CASPER

CHALERMCHAI CHARUVASTR

PATRICK T CHITWOOD

PAUL J CHITWOOD

RAJAN CHOPRA

THOMAS J CLASBY 3rd

IAN A CLOSE

J CLYNK

PETER J COCCARO

FRANK O COCHRANE

BRYAN J COLLIER

ALEX COLMAN

DAVID B COOK

HAROLD COOPER

PATRICK A COSTA

PHILIPPE COTIN

JOHN CWETLER

WOLFGANG CWETLER

LUDWIG H DAHL

KIYOSHI DAIMATSU

RENE DALLA CORTE

MATS DANIELSSON

THOMAS H DAVIS

GLENN G DEBONA

PAUL F DEIHLE

JAMES F DELEONE

MICHAEL DENKENSOHN

CECIL L DeVAULT

ROLAND F DIETRICH

JAMES M B DIGNAN

ALLAN N DISHINGTON

DEREK L DONLON

GEORGE F DOUGHTIE

HARRY E DOYLE

STIG DRAPKIN

AXEL C DUBS

NORMAN McL DUNCAN

RONALD L DUNN

JACKSON L DURKEE

SCOTT G DWECK

PETER C EBELL

ROBERT J ERCEBACH

CHRISTER ERIKSSON

ARTHUR FAHEY

ROBERT E FARRELL

SION A FAULK

WILLIAM T FEHERTY

BARRY A FERGUSON

WILLIAM FINLAY

JOHN P FLANNERY

ROBERT W FLIPPEN

PHILIP FLUITMAN

JOHN W FOX

RICHARD D FRAME

A T FRIETMAN

JAMES B GALLACHER

DENNIS J GALLAGHER

MICHAEL D GALLAGHER

PATRICK J GALLAGHER
JOESEPH P GANLEY
JOHN A GELLMANN
RUNE GENNERUD
KOHEI GODA
LEE GOODMAN
PETER J GORDON
ROBERT D GRANT
LEIF GUSTAFSSON
LIONEL HAGUE
ROY A HALPIN
ROGER W HAMBLIN
ROBERT HANCOCK
TSUNEO HARADA
F PAUL HARGARTEN
NORMAN L HARRIS
YASUO HASHIMOTO
GEORGE HENNINGER
RICHARD J HERRMAN
SIGEL J HOFFMAN
GEORGE E HOLDING
L D HOMBROEK
JUN GI HONG
HIROYUKI HOTTA
PATRICK W HOWE
MICHAEL HUERNER
TOMOHIKO IKEDA
RICHARD C IRWIN SNR
TATSUNORI ISHIMARU
EDWARD J JOFFE
CLARENCE JOHNSON
MALCOLM JOHNSTON
DORAN A JONES
KIM JONGSHIN
GEORGE KATAOKA
AKIRA KAWANISHI
SUGURU KAWANISHI
LEO J KELLY, M.D.
THOMAS KIS
LONNIE J KNOWLES
WALTER KOGEL
GYLFI KRISTINSSON
LASZLO KRONHEIM
PIETER KUHNE
KIL HYUN LEE
ROBERT M LENIHAN
THOMAS LEON
HARALD LINDSTOEL
JOHN D LOCH
HERBERT R LOCKE
RONALD LOMAS

RONALD C LOPEZ
IAN LORIMER
RICHARD R LOVE
TOM LYNCH
TOM D Mac KINNON
ALLAN D B MacDONALD
JOSEPH D MACHIA
D KEITH MacKENZIE
JOHN S MADARAS JNR M.D.
SABURO MAEDA
JERRY MANSKE
ALEXANDER C MARTIN
BRUCE MARTIN
ROSS MATHESON
AKITAKA MATSUBARA
SIDNEY L MATTHEW
MATS MATTIASSON
KENNETH G MC CUDDEN
PAUL McCUTCHEON
WILLIAM T McEWAN, JNR
VICTOR McGAVIN
KEN MCKEE
ALEXANDER B McKENZIE
GARY B McKENZIE
JAMES F McLISTER
JOHN I McNISH
GERALD MILLAR
LANDON C G MILLER
TOSHIO MISHIMA
SHOZO MIZUNO
HARUO MORIYAMA
WAYNE P MORRONI
HANS J MUELLER
YASUHIRO MURAOKA
DANIEL E MUSCHOLT
WOLFGANG R NEUMANN
CHESTER L NOBLETT
ATSUSHI OHMATSU
HIDEAKI OKADA
ISAMU OKAZAKI
MORTON W OLMAN
GORAN J OLSSON
MICHAEL B OPPENHEIM
ALVIN ORLIAN
B M ORTH
WILLIAM J OSCROFT
ERIC OSTER
GILBERT PAPAZIAN
EDGAR M PATCH
MIKE PECK
WILLIAM W PENDLETON JNR

BERT A PERLE
KENT PETERSON
JOSEPH E POIST
PAUL PRYOR
NEIL RABITOY
M LARS RASTMAN
BERND REUMANN
JEFFREY B ROBERTS
HENRIK ROBERTSON
THOS ROHR
NAT G ROSASCO
FRANK ROSS
HENDRIK ROZEMEYER
KO SAKOTA
JAN SANDIN
KYOICHI SASAKI
HIROSHI SATO
KLAUS SCHULZE
HANS SCHUMACHER
NORMAN O SEAGRAM
RAYMOND SHARPE
LAWRENCE R SHEEHAN
PETER A E SHONIKER
MORGAN SHUMBA
ANDREW SIMPSON
ROBERT S SLOAN
A L SMITH
RONALD C SMITH
FOREST G SMITH JNR
THOMAS D SNYDER
MARTIN SODERBERG
SOREN C SOMMERFELT
STANLEY R SOSZKA
WOLFGANG SPANNAGEL
WILLIAM A SPARROW
G WILLIAM SPINDLER
JAY B SPITZER
JOHN D ST. CLAIR
LOUIS STAIANO
LOUIS STAINO
JOHN STAVER
RICHARD STEED
DONALD V STIRLING
JOHN S STONE
RAY C STORMONT
JOHN STRAWN
ROY STROTHERS
KEIZO SUGITA
MAKOTO SUZUKI
TOMOYUKI SUZUKI
MAKOTO TAGUCHI

MIKE TAKEMORI
CHARLES R TAYLOR
P R TAYLOR III
FREDERICK G TERRY III
LEON M THOMPSON
WILLIAM A B THOMSON
KUNIO TOIDA
OSKAY TOYGAR
GARY D TRAVERS
EISUKE TSUKAMOTO
ROBERT R TUPPER
JOHN VALLEY
HANS VAN DER SCHAAF
THOMAS A VANDERSLICE
CCH VERMEER
PIETER A VERMEER
GABRIELE VILLA
W IAN VOGAN
MARTIN WAGEN
ARTHUR J WALLS
WINFRIED H WALTER
ALEXANDER M WATT
CARL L WEARE
CLEMENS WEGNER
ROBERT A WEISGERBER
GERD H K WEITBRECHT
J WILLIAM WHALE
PETER WIDINGHOFF
DAVID WILKIE
BILL WILLS
JEFFREY T WILSON
PETER J WOITOWICH
MIKIO YAMAMOTO
SHIGERU YAMASHITA
AKIHIKO YAMAZAKI
HANS D ZIEGLER
MICHAEL I ZUFLACHT

142

JUVENILE MEMBERS 1992

ANDREW P AYTON	GRAEME N FINLAY	SCOTT LEE	PETER G T STEWART
ALAN J CAMPBELL	MURRAY GARLAND	RYAN G LUMSDEN	ROBERT A TAYLOR
GARETH D CLARK	STUART B GILMOUR	EWAN MARRONEY	ROSS C THOM
DAVID COLGAN	BILLY GREENWOOD	RUAIRIDH McQUEEN	BRUNO WILLIAMS
COLIN DONALDSON	SEAN GREENWOOD JNR	PAUL MURNIN	DUNCAN J WYSE
PAUL T DONALDSON	ANDREW G HENDERSON	MARTYN RABBITT	
JAMIE K DOUGLAS	MARC AUREL A HUEBNER	LEE ROWAN	
GRAEME R EDIE	ALEXANDER P KEOGH	JAMES RUSSELL	
MICHAEL S EDIE	AJAY KUMAR	ROBERT W STEVEN	

JUNIOR MEMBERS 1992

ANDREW J AITKEN	ROSS G DUNCAN	KEVIN LIDDLE	SCOTT SIEVEWRIGHT
ROSS ARROLL	MICHAEL C ELDER	NEIL E LUMSDEN	IAN B STEVEN
ALAN G BAIRD	ALAN J ERSKINE	COLIN N R MALCOLM	NEIL M STEVEN
ALASTAIR BARRON	DANIEL J FAIRLIE	JAMES R MARTIN	JAMES D STEWART
KEVIN C BROADFOOT	CHRISTOPHER J FALCONER	CAMPBELL McNEILL	STEVEN STEWART
JAMES T BUNCH	DAVID B FINLAY	DAVID R MITCHELL	ROBERT J SUTTIE
RICHARD BUNCH	RORY J FYFE	STEVEN P MURRAY	DUGALD A THOM
GORDON M BUNTIN	JAMIE A GRIEVE	JOHN A NORMAND	LEWIS J WILLIAMSON
SCOTT L BURNETT	BRIAN C HEGGIE	GEORGE OLVER	GILLES A WILSON
GARY CARGILL	MALCOLM J JACK	BEN PACHOLEK	
DAVID M CLARK	NEILL KEMP	HOWARD PALSAY	
RODERICK A CLARK	KEVIN KIRK	IAN PALSAY	
SCOTT COLLINGTON	STEVEN R LATTO	ANDREW S M PATRICK	
GORDON S CRAM	EDWARD H LEE	STEPHEN J RICHARDSON	
DAVID A CRICHTON	MALCOLM A S LEIPER	STUART RUSSELL	
CHRISTOPHER DOUGLAS	DARREN LIDDLE	MURRAY SCOTT	

LIFE MEMBERS 1992

GEORGE BAIRD	WILLIAM W FENTON	WILLIAM MENZIES	ANDREW T SOUTAR
JOHN B BERRY	A JANNETTA	KENNETH RAMSAY	FREDERICK J STURROCK
JAMES M BLACK	ROBERT B JOLLY	WILLIAM P ROBERTSON	W WILKINSON
JOHN A BRAID	DUNCAN L JOY	WILLIAM S SIMPSON	

OUR SESQUICENTENNIAL YEAR

These words are penned in November 1992 with our sesquicentennial year only weeks away.

They may be helpful to the writer of the Bi-centenary History in 2043 in giving him details of the years' events.

In January we will display the "new" Club flag based on the description of our first Club flag in the Minute of 23rd January 1852. At the same ceremony we will show an oil painting of our first captain David Todd. This was painted by John Cairns. There will also be a series of prints of our Open Champions drawn by David Joy.

We plan to repeat the Married men v Single men match played in July 1880. Despite having three Open Champions in the team, the Married men lost.

There will be a Midnight Match commemorating the one played in April 1887 when J.O.F. Morris played three club members by lantern light.

A long Driving Competition will be organised similar to the one described in a May 1895 Minute. This was won by W. Anderson with a drive of 220 yards. My suggestion that we include a Shortest Drive Competition has met with no support!

On Monday 21st July there will be a Pro Am tournament on the Old Course. The Club also has the courtesy of the Old Course on Sunday 22nd August. One hundred and fifty St. Andrews Golf Club members will be playing a composite team made up of representatives of all the Fife Golf Clubs and these clubs which have annual fixtures with us.

A match will be played against a team from Leven reminding us of our first ever Club match in November 1849. Another match will be with the Thistle Golf Club. Our first recorded match with them is dated July 1890.

Our formal celebratory Dinner will be held in the Town Hall on Friday 24th September and an informal dance is scheduled for 29th October.

The final event in our one hundred and fiftieth year will take place after the November A.G.M. Regularly, last century, our A.G.M's were followed with the eating of 3d pies and an evening of song and entertainment. There will be 3d pies and Victorian songs on the programme for that evening.

It looks as if 1993 may be a happy and memorable year for us all.